GRIEF
ONE DAY
at a TIME

In partnership with
McInnis & Holloway
Funeral Home
I hope that in this book
you find comfort and
understanding
in this daily companion

Alan D. Wolfelt

Companion
PRESS

Companion Press is dedicated to the education and support of both the bereaved and bereavement caregivers. We believe that those who companion the bereaved by walking with them as they journey in grief have a wondrous opportunity: to help others embrace and grow through grief—and to lead fuller, more deeply-lived lives themselves because of this important ministry.

For a complete catalog and ordering information, write, call, or visit:

Companion Press | The Center for Loss and Life Transition
3735 Broken Bow Road | Fort Collins, CO 80526
(970) 226-6050 | www.centerforloss.com

GRIEF
ONE DAY
at a TIME

365 meditations to help you heal after loss

ALAN D. WOLFELT, PH.D.

Companion Press is an imprint of the Center for Loss and Life Transition, 3735 Broken Bow Road, Fort Collins, Colorado 80526.

24 23 22 21 20 19 18 17   5 4

ISBN: 978-1-61722-238-2

*With an eternity of gratitude I dedicate this book
to my three precious children: Megan, Christopher, and Jaimie.
They are among my most important teachers in this life. Bless you for
what you have given me in this life and may I someday live up
to what you deserve in a father and mentor.*

WELCOME

Grief is what we think and feel inside after someone we love dies, and it is an every-day experience.

That is, when we are grieving a significant loss, we feel our grief every single day. We wake up each morning knowing that today we will experience hurt and an ever-changing mixture of painful thoughts and feelings.

Grief's very relentlessness is often frustrating, challenging, and exhausting.

Our hope lies in small, daily doses of mourning.

Mourning is when we express our grief outside ourselves. While grief is internal, mourning is external. Talking about our thoughts and feelings, crying, journaling, participating in a support group—these and other expressive activities help us begin to integrate our grief.

Yes, our grief is a daily challenge. But if we actively mourn, each day in grief can also bring a small measure of healing. Encountering and engaging with our thoughts and feelings softens them. Mourning one day at a time brings healing one day at a time.

I encourage you to read the daily entries and accompanying meditations when you awaken each morning. Doing so may bolster your courage to grieve and mourn authentically throughout the day ahead.

Thank you for entrusting me to walk alongside you on this 365 day journey. Such companionship is essential in grief. I hope we meet in person one day.

Alan D. Wolfelt

JANUARY 1

"At the rising of the sun and at its going down,
We remember them.
At the blowing of the wind and in the chill of winter,
We remember them.
At the opening of buds and in the rebirth of spring,
We remember them.

At the rustling of leaves and in the beauty of autumn,
We remember them.
In the beginning of the year and when it ends,
We remember them.
So long as we live, they too shall live for they are now a part of us as
We remember them."

—Excerpt, by Sylvan Kamens and Rabbi Jack Riemer

At this transition from the old year to the new, we think about
those we love who have died. A year they will not enjoy.
A year they will not be here for us. A year—
at once so swift and so excruciatingly slow.

But in this new year, we will remember them,
and we will love them. And those are the two
most powerful forces in the universe.

This year, I will remember, and I will love.

JANUARY 2

"And now we welcome the new year,
full of things that have never been."
— Rainer Maria Rilke

We who grieve may not exactly feel like celebrating the new year, but we can sometimes feel a bit of relief that the last calendar year—which was rough—is over.

The new year holds the promise of a clean slate. It offers opportunities for new beginnings. It whispers of hope.

Let us welcome hope whenever and wherever and whyever we feel it stir. And as we slog forward into this new year, let us try to remember that it will be full of things that have never been. It will lack special people, yes, but it will also bring surprises—gifts, joys, love, and, if we continue to do our hard work of active mourning, a measure of healing.

I can both mourn and expect good things
to happen in this new year.

JANUARY 3

"On this bald hill the new year hones its edge.

Faceless and pale as china

The round sky goes on minding its business.

Your absence is inconspicuous;

Nobody can tell what I lack."

— Sylvia Plath

Part of what makes grief so hard is that it's invisible. Inside we are torn apart, but outside we look basically the same. Nobody can tell what we lack—sometimes not even the people who are closest to us.

In times gone by, mourners wore black clothing or special jewelry to alert others to their grief. We too can wear a symbol of our loss, such as an armband, a photo button, or, as we do here at the Center for Loss, an "Under Reconstruction" pin. Or we can simply make it a point to be forthcoming with the people in our lives, letting them know what happened and sharing our current thoughts and feelings. We can appropriately communicate our lack.

When others ask me how I am doing, I will not say, "fine" unless I am truly fine. Instead, I will learn to share my inner reality so that I am living and communicating my truth.

JANUARY 4

"Nothing makes a room feel emptier than wanting somebody in it."
— Author Unknown

Oh, the pain of missing those who have died. The memories are there, the love is still there, but the physical presence is…gone. Forever. Even though it has been 16 years since my father died, I still have moments when I remember that I will never again see him on this earth, and I gasp aloud at the hurt of the realization.

Our five senses ascertain reality. We see, hear, touch, smell, and taste our world. When we are missing someone, we may still be able to touch an article of their clothing, breathe in the scent of their pillow, and see and hear them on cherished videos. I call these "linking objects" because they link us to the physical presence we are missing so much. Linking objects soothe, honor, and help us transition to a relationship of memory in lieu of presence.

I wish you were here. Right here, where I could see, touch, and hear you. I will always miss you, but I will also always love you. The love is still here.

JANUARY 5

"In the bleak midwinter, frosty wind made moan.
Earth stood hard as iron, water like a stone."

— Christina Rossetti

Where I live in Colorado, winter can be brutal. January is dark
and can be bitter cold. The wind at my home in the foothills of
the Rocky Mountains slices like a knife. Snow and ice cover
the iron ground, making driving and even
walking outside treacherous.

Midwinter is a time to withdraw and to grieve. It is a time to
huddle indoors, sit by the fire, and contemplate the meaning of
life and death. It is also a time for hot chocolate and meaningful
conversations with people we care about. We can heed grief's call
for stillness and also share this time of reflection with others.

Midwinter can be a time to take a break, too! More and more
as I get older, I like to carve out time in January for a vacation
somewhere warm. But even when I can't travel, I can still
visit a friend's house, go to my favorite restaurant,
or spend time just being.

We grieve and withdraw. We take breaks for warmth and relief.
This is the January of our grief.

On the bleakest days, I will remember that withdrawing
is necessary, that talking to others helps, and that
I need breaks now and then.

JANUARY 6

"Journal writing is a voyage to the interior."
— Christina Baldwin

When we write about our grief in a journal, we're expressing our thoughts and feelings outside of ourselves. That means journaling is a form of mourning, and it can help us heal.

There are no rules for grief journaling, but you might consider jotting down your thoughts and feelings first thing when you wake up or each night before you go to sleep. You can use a paper journal or a computer. Entries can be as long or as short as you want. Don't worry about what you're writing or how well you're writing it. Just write whatever's on your mind and heart.

Over time, journaling also helps us see our progress. When we go back and reread things we wrote months ago, we notice the ways in which our grief has changed and softened. Sometimes seeing how far we've already come helps us keep going.

If I'm not already a journaler, I'll give it a try today.
I just might like it.

JANUARY 7

"You don't get explanations in real life. You just get moments that are absolutely, utterly, inexplicably odd."

— Neil Gaiman

In grief we often look for explanations. Why did the people we love have to die? Why now? Why in this way?
Why am I still here and they are not?

It's normal and necessary to ask such questions. Grief is a spiritual journey, and asking—and searching for answers to— the big meaning-of-life questions is definitely on the itinerary.

We don't always find answers. Lots of times we end up shrugging and surrendering to the mystery. We find ways to trust in the chaos. Life is odd. But like so many things that are odd, it's also beautiful because of its idiosyncratic nature.
Tidy explanations are overrated.

I can look for explanations, but I might end up finding a sort of peace in not finding them.

JANUARY 8

"Everything is falling together perfectly, even though it looks as if some things are falling apart. Trust in the process you are now experiencing."

— Neale Donald Walsch

Grief is a long, winding road. It is a process, not a moment in time. And when we are in the middle of the journey, it can seem like we are not making any progress. In fact, it can feel like things are falling more and more apart.

In grief, things often do get worse before they get better. When it feels like everything is falling apart, we must remind ourselves that actually, everything is as it should be. As long as we are doing the work of encountering and expressing our grief, we can trust that everything is falling together perfectly. It may not seem like it at any given moment, but all is well. We can trust in the process we are experiencing.

Today I will allow my grief to become mourning, and no matter what happens, I will trust that the journey is leading me toward healing.

JANUARY 9

*"I like these cold, gray winter days. Days like these
let you savor a bad mood."*

— Bill Watterson

We must admit that most of us enjoy a bad mood now and then. It's satisfying to grump and complain, to close ourselves up, even to slam the occasional door.

I think we get some satisfaction out of bad moods because we recognize that they're necessary. In fact, they're not really "bad" moods at all—they're just a different flavor of mood Feelings are never good or bad; they just *are*.

We could never revel in our loss; we would undo it if we could! But since we can't, we can indulge our "bad moods" whenever we feel like it. We can withdraw and grouse and have a good cry. We can feel sorry for ourselves and throw a self-pity party. Because when we do these things, we're simply acknowledging our reality and embracing our pain—both tasks we have to undertake on the road to healing.

When I'm in a "bad mood," I'll wallow in it if I feel like it.

JANUARY 10

"Pain is the doorway to wisdom and to truth."
— Keith Miller

The word "January" comes from the Roman god of doorways, Janus (after the Etruscan word *janua*, which means door). He had charge of the gates of Heaven as well as all doorways and gates, physical and metaphorical. He is often depicted as having two faces—one looking forward and one looking backward.

Our grief is like that. We look back at the past we shared with the people who died, and we look forward at a future without them. Like Janus, we are standing in the doorway, but this doorway of our grief is not a comfortable place to be. We're betwixt and between, in what is called "liminal space." *Limina* is the Latin word for threshold and is related to the concept of limbo.

We don't like being in this limbo doorway. We would rather go backward to the way things were or fast forward to some future time in which we're feeling settled again. But here's the thing: it is only in the doorway of liminal space that we can reconstruct our shattered worldviews and re-emerge as transformed, whole people who are ready to live fully again.

I don't like this doorway of grief, but I'm learning to respect it.

JANUARY 11

"It is in our idleness, in our dreams, that the submerged truth sometimes comes to the top."
— Virginia Woolf

When the lethargy of grief overtakes us, we can feel as if we are moving through mud. Everything takes too much effort. We are tired physically, cognitively, emotionally, socially, and spiritually.

This is normal and necessary, but sometimes we rebuke ourselves or feel guilty for being so lazy. Instead, we should flip the rebuke over and see that sometimes it is our very idleness that allows progress in our healing. The lethargy of grief nurtures our need to slow down, turn inward, and bask in being in neutral. Times of not doing and simply be-ing can allow us to discover new insights and experience breakthroughs.

In our stillness, the truth may rise to the top.

Today I will revel in any idleness I may find myself experiencing. I may even set aside time for idleness.

JANUARY 12

"Hard times arouse an instinctive desire for authenticity."
— Coco Chanel

Grief has a way of cutting to the chase. Pretenses fall away. We find that we want nothing to do with phoniness. We don't have the energy for fakery, and besides, it suddenly seems so pointless, even distasteful.

Our newfound (or intensified) instinct for authenticity is borne of our grief. We've lost someone who gave our life meaning. That loss has made us keenly aware of what is meaningful to us and what is not. It's like turning on a black light in an otherwise dark room; certain things become obvious that we couldn't see clearly before.

The good news is that we can use this time of grieving to jettison habits, belongings, and even people we now realize do not resonate with our inner truth. If something seems ungenuine, or we simply don't care about it anymore, out it goes. This winnowing process is valuable and has the power to make the rest of our lives richer and more meaningful.

I'm going to pay attention to what really matters to me. Everything else I will let fall by the wayside.

JANUARY 13

"Be yourself. Everyone else is already taken."
— Oscar Wilde

We are all mourners, but no two of us are traveling the exact same grief journey. Our grief is unique, shaped by our one-of-a-kind histories, personalities, relationships with the people who died, spiritual or religious backgrounds, circumstances of the death, support systems, and other factors.

We'll grieve as only we would grieve, and we need to mourn in ways that work for us. When others tell us we must do this or that, we have the right to ignore them.

I'll be myself in grief, and you be yourself.
Everybody else is already taken.

I'll be myself in grief. My gut instincts will tell me what's right for me and what's not.

JANUARY 14

"What's past is prologue."
— William Shakespeare

Leave it to Shakespeare to capture such a profound life lesson in just four words. Often we grievers are encouraged to "just move on." We are told to "let go," "get past it," and "put the past in the past." Our culture has been contaminated by an insidious misconception that emotional-spiritual pain is bad and that we should simply "forget" any past experiences that are now causing us pain.

Hogwash. Our pasts are the prologues to our futures. First of all, we *can't* forget: our brains aren't wired that way. And second, we shouldn't *want* to forget! Our memories house our very existence. They inform and give context to who we are today. Memories of past relationships, especially, are our most meaningful treasures.

Yes, today is the first day of the rest of your life, and you do have the power to create the future you desire. But your past will always be a significant part of who you are tomorrow.

I will remember you. You are an important part of who I am today and will remain an important part of me in every tomorrow.

JANUARY 15

"During a panic attack, I remember that today is just today, and that is all that it is. I take a deep breath in, and I realize that in this moment I am fine and everything is OK."

— Max Greenfield

It's thought that about ten percent of us experience panic attacks at least occasionally. Panic attacks are sudden, overwhelming feelings of intense fear, complete with symptoms like shortness of breath, sweatiness, heart palpitations, shaking, and anxiety about losing control or even dying. They commonly come on without warning and in situations that, on the surface at least, seem safe or normal.

Essentially, panic attacks are misfirings of our built-in fight-or-flight systems. They're now known to be triggered by cues, internal and external, that our brains interpret as "danger!" The natural fears and worries we experience in grief can act as such cues. In fact, in grief, panic attacks are often invitations to go backward and explore any aspects of our loss that make us feel fearful or anxious.

If you're suffering from panic attacks, I urge you to see a licensed therapist who can help you explore them and get them under control. Until you find ways to tame your panic attacks or intense fears, you will not have the focus or sense of safety you need to grieve, mourn, and heal.

If I'm feeling panicky or suffering panic attacks, that simply means I need help calming my body's fight-or-flight system.

JANUARY 16

"'But I don't want to go among mad people,' Alice remarked.
'Oh, you can't help that,' said the Cat. 'We're all mad here.'"
— Lewis Carroll

Most of us feel crazy at some point in our grief journeys.
After all, it's a mad place to be.

We don't want to be here, but here we are.

The really crazy thing is, crazy is normal in grief.
Loss upends us, and we realize that our lives will never
fully return to the mostly stable, sensical version of reality
we thought we inhabited. Now we know:
It's human existence that's crazy—not our grief.

Today I'll remember that we're all mad here.
Beauty, love, and joy live in the madness too.

JANUARY 17

"Guilt isn't always a rational thing, Clio realized. Guilt is a weight that will crush you whether you deserve it or not."

— Maureen Johnson

We grievers tend to be good at guilt.

We may feel guilty that someone else died and we are still alive. We might feel guilty when we catch ourselves experiencing moments of happiness, reasoning that the person who died deserves our unflagging sadness. We can feel guilty about bad things that happened in our relationships with the people who died. We may feel guilty about things we did or didn't do that we imagine may have contributed to the death somehow—however irrational this thinking might be. And in cases of lingering death, such as from cancer, we often feel guilty about the relief we feel.

We can't simply dismiss our guilt, though. Like all our other thoughts and feelings, our guilt isn't right or wrong—it simply *is*. And because it exists, we need to find ways to express it. That's how to soften guilt—expressing it outside of ourselves until we mostly don't feel it anymore.

If I feel guilty about something that has to do with the person who died, it doesn't mean I actually am to blame. But it does mean I need to talk to good listeners about it.

JANUARY 18

"Your body is precious. It is your vehicle for awakening.
Treat it with care."
— Buddha

We feel our grief in our bodies. We may have headaches, stomachaches, back pain, heartburn, or other common symptoms. We may feel short of breath, nauseated, or generally "not good." We're more likely to come down with viruses. We may not be eating or sleeping well.

All of these grief symptoms are really signals that we need to give attention to our need to mourn. But it's hard to do our necessary grief work if we're not feeling well physically.

The answer lies in focusing first on good self-care. We must eat nutritious foods and exercise, at least lightly, most days. We must drink six tall glasses of water each day, because we are at risk for dehydration. Rest is especially important. We must lay our bodies down two to three times a day for 20 minutes, even if we are not able to fall sleep. If insomnia is an ongoing problem, we need to see our doctors; we simply cannot mourn well if we're not sleeping well.

I will make good physical self-care a priority
because it's integral to my healing.

JANUARY 19

"Nothing resembles selfishness more closely than self-respect."
— George Sand

Especially early in our grief, we may find ourselves deaf to the needs of others. We may not want to listen to other people's problems. We may not have the energy to attend to our children or other family members (who may also be grieving). We often feel flabbergasted that the world is still turning while our lives are at complete standstills.

Are we being self-indulgent? Are we too wrapped up in ourselves? Has grief turned us into narcissistic egomaniacs?

Actually, the temporary selfishness of grief is a form of self-respect. When all we can think about is how we are feeling, it's because we've been torn apart and need to work on putting ourselves back together before we can be of use to others. Our self-focus honors this reality. I call it the "cocooning phenomenon," and it's normal and necessary.

Think of it like the smart advice to put on your own oxygen mask first in the event of an airplane catastrophe. If you don't, you'll conk out completely, and then what good are you to yourself or to anyone else?

I must attend to my own grief right now. I am the priority.

JANUARY 20

*"We think that the point is to pass the test or overcome the problem,
but the truth is that things don't really get solved. They come together
and they fall apart. Then they come together again and fall apart
again...The healing comes from letting there be room for all of this to
happen: room for grief, for relief, for misery, for joy."*

— Pema Chodron

Oh how we wish we could solve our grief. If only we could
fix it, cure it, resolve it. Just make it go away.

Wouldn't it be something if we could feel only our love
for those who have died and none of the hurt?

Alas, that's not how being human works. We can't cure our
grief; we can only become reconciled to it. We can only
learn to integrate it into our continued living.

The healing comes not from eliminating the pain but from
making room for the pain. When we accommodate the hurt,
we also create space for new love and joy.

*I am starting to embrace the understanding that things come
together then fall apart then come together again. There is room
in my life for all of this to happen.*

JANUARY 21

"I wouldn't live with me, believe me. I'm moody."
— Mario Cantone

Lots of us find ourselves moody in grief, even if we weren't particularly temperamental people before. Our mood changes can be subtle or dramatic. They can be triggered by a familiar place, a song, an insensitive comment, or even a change in the weather.

I think our moods are simply our grief talking to us. Much in the same way that fluctuating hormones can make the emotions of teenagers and pregnant women volatile, our grief courses through our minds, bodies, and souls, spiking at seemingly random moments.

When we notice our fickle feelings flare, let's try to be patient and understanding with ourselves. We can embrace and experience each new mood as it arises while at the same time maintaining a calm awareness that the feeling is normal and temporary. In other words, we can both ride the rollercoaster and stand on the sidelines, watching ourselves ride the rollercoaster. A mindfulness trick that takes practice, this can help us feel a sense of peace even in the middle of our naturally mercurial mourning.

When I'm moody, I'm moody. It's OK.

JANUARY 22

"Grief is not a disorder, a disease, or a sign of weakness. It is an emotional, physical, and spiritual necessity, the price you pay for love. The only cure for grief is to grieve."

— Rabbi Earl Grollman

Sometimes we think of our grief as a problem to be solved. We are in pain, and we need to find a way to make the pain go away, as if our grief is a headache or a sore shoulder. But our grief is not a problem or disorder. It is not something to try to get rid of or go around. It is not bad. Instead, we must understand that grief is as much a part of life as love.

Grief is not a problem to be fixed. It is a normal and necessary spiritual journey that can only be experienced. Yes, it is painful and challenging, but fully exploring and expressing the pain is the only way through.

Life is love. Life is grief. May I have the courage to embrace both when they come my way.

JANUARY 23

"You do not need to know precisely what is happening, or exactly where it is all going. What you need is to recognize the possibilities and challenges offered by the present moment, and to embrace them with courage, faith, and hope."

— Thomas Merton

This living in the present moment stuff can seem like nonsense. Especially when we're grieving, we find ourselves constantly thinking about the past. We also seem to worry endlessly about the future. And the present? It hurts, that's what. Nowhere is there a reprieve.

Except. Except maybe we can find an oasis of peace in the present moment. First of all, sometimes we can distract ourselves in the here and now with entertainment such as browsing online or watching TV. We need such breaks from our grief every day. Second, we can embrace our memories, thoughts, and feelings as they arise. In the present moment, we can and need to actively engage with the pain of our grief.

But third, we can also face the now with courage, faith, and hope. Yes, the present moment hurts, but it is also alive with possibilities. In grief, every new minute harbors a paradox: we mourn, but we also live. We can learn to do both.

I will actively mourn today AND work on embracing each new moment with courage, faith, and hope.

JANUARY 24

"January is the quietest month in the garden… But just because it looks quiet doesn't mean that nothing is happening. The soil, open to the sky, absorbs the pure rainfall, while micro-organisms convert tilled-under fodder into usable nutrients for the next crop of plants. The feasting earthworms tunnel along, aerating the soil and preparing it to welcome the seeds and bare roots to come."

— Rosalie Muller Wright

When our grief has gone outwardly quiet and we have withdrawn to the deepest parts of ourselves, it may seem like nothing is happening. Like we are making no progress.

But the necessary turning inward of grief is not truly stasis. Things are happening in our minds, hearts, and souls. We are remembering. We are working through challenging questions about the meaning of life and death. We are thinking and feeling. We are struggling with our spirituality.

Soon we will need to share our grief outside of ourselves. We will need to mourn. But when we are quietest, we are preparing for the active mourning and healing to come.

When my grief goes quiet, it means I am doing the necessary work of turning inward.

JANUARY 25

*"Be gentle with yourself. You are a child of the universe, no less than
the trees and the stars. In the noisy confusion of life,
keep peace in your soul."*

— Max Ehrmann

We are each of us a child of the universe. We are all unique
masterpieces. Our bodies are inhabited by one-of-a-kind souls.
Just by being born, we claimed our singular, glorious place in
the constellation of humanity.

We are wont to remember our own divinity when we are
grieving. Our grief can make us feel small and insignificant. It
ravages our self-esteem. It diminishes us.

But grief's destructiveness is merely an illusion. Yes, our earthly
lives are torn apart right now and our souls are hurting, but
truly our grief does not—cannot—touch the unalterable fact
of our timeless existence. Deep within our hurting souls is an
inextinguishable flame of eternal glory and peace.

*I am a child of the universe. In the noisy confusion of my grief,
I am learning to keep peace in my soul.*

JANUARY 26

"Helplessness is such a rotten feeling. There's nothing you can do about it. Being helpless is like being paralyzed. It's sickness. The cure calls for a monumental effort to stand up and start walking somewhere, anywhere. But that takes some doing."

— Chuck Barris

The helplessness of grief is a rotten feeling. While part of us realizes we had no control over what happened, another part feels a sense of powerlessness at not having been able to prevent it. We would like to have our lives back the way they were, but we can't. We feel helpless over the way things are happening. Our grief paralyzes us.

Our feelings of helplessness aren't really sickness, though; they're normal and natural. And surrendering to the reality that we are not in control is part of our grief work. But when we're ready, we can also take action. We can stand up and start walking somewhere, anywhere.

We can and we must activate our grief, transforming it into mourning. We can't control what happens in our lives, but we can control what we *do* about it. It's a monumental effort, all right, but it's also transformative. We can be powerful in our powerlessness.

I feel so helpless. Yet I can stand up and start walking somewhere, anywhere.

JANUARY 27

"Things to do today:

1. Get up.

2. Survive.

3. Go back to bed."

— Author Unknown

Some days in grief are survival days. If we manage simply to get through the day, we've accomplished a lot.

Not every day can be about "progress" or "moving forward." Some days are about struggling to keep from falling back. Others are about backsliding like crazy.

Something transformative happens when we survive such days. We learn that we *can* survive such days. And that fact bolsters our confidence for whatever comes next. We're not in control of our grief or of our lives, but we're learning there is a measure of peace in learning to go with the flow.

I will survive today. Some days that is enough.

JANUARY 28

"Sometimes I just cry without knowing why."

— Author Unknown

Sometimes we cry when we're thinking about the person who died. Crying is good. Tears help us release our pent-up feelings. But there's also another kind of crying I call "borrowed tears." These are tears that spring up when we are touched by something random we see, hear, touch, taste, or smell, and we react with strong emotion. Borrowed tears often seem to come out of nowhere and are triggered by something we don't associate with the person who died and wouldn't normally have been upset by.

Borrowed tears are called what they are called because we seem to be "borrowing" them from someone else's store of pain and memory. They're not ours! We might find ourselves crying at a sappy commercial on TV or seeing a little bird out our window. These things never made us sad before. Why are we crying now?

We're crying because our hearts and souls are hurting and our emotions are tender. Think of it this way: If you press on your leg gently with your hand, it doesn't hurt. But if you break your leg and then press on it, even the slightest touch can hurt. Our hearts are broken now, and anything that touches our hearts even slightly may hurt them. This is normal and will pass as our hearts are healed.

I can borrow tears whenever I need them.
I'll give them back when I'm done with them.

JANUARY 29

"Don't believe in miracles. Depend on them."
— Laurence J. Peter

Lots of us grievers depend on our beliefs in certain miracles. They're the only things that keep us going.

We might believe that we have received signs from the person who died. We might believe that the person who died is now having a great time with family members and friends who died before him. We might believe that the death somehow saved others' lives here on earth.

Thank goodness for miracles.
Let's keep our eyes open for more of them.

My relationship with the person who died was a miracle. That's all the proof I need to embrace all the other miracles that may come my way.

JANUARY 30

*"Make it dark, make it grim, make it tough, but then,
for the love of God, tell a joke."*

— Joss Whedon

Grief is dark and grim and tough. We've got a lot of hard, sad work to do in this darkness. There ain't no gettin' around that fact.

Still, we need to pop into the light now and then. We need jokes. We need laughter. We need levity. For the love of God, we need bursts of sunshine.

Our healing begins to unfold when we repeatedly and actively find ways to embrace the darkness. But healing also requires daily doses of light. Dark, dark, dark, light! Dark, light, dark, light! It's the back-and-forth that keeps us alive.

*I need to laugh sometimes. I need to be entertained and
set aside my loss for a while.*

JANUARY 31

"When you get to the end of your rope, tie a knot and hang on."

— Franklin D. Roosevelt

Sometimes our grief has us at the ends of our ropes. We feel like we've used up our last reserves of coping and grace, and we can't hold on any longer.

Good ol' FDR has a suggestion. When we're at the ends of our ropes, we can *do* something. Instead of continuing to be passively buffeted about by all the bad stuff that life seems to be sending our way, we can act. Instead of just clinging, we can reach out and tie a knot.

In grief, tying a knot might mean phoning a friend. Or making an appointment to see a compassionate grief counselor. Or taking a time-out to visit a place we find spiritual. Or attending a support group. We can't make our losses go away, but we can tie a knot.

If ever I feel I'm at the end of my rope, I'll tie a knot.

FEBRUARY 1

"Life is not orderly. No matter how we try to make life so, right in the middle of it we die, lose a leg, fall in love, drop a jar of applesauce. In summer, we work hard to make a tidy garden, bordered by pansies with rows or clumps of columbine, petunias, bleeding hearts. Then we find ourselves longing for the forest, where everything has the appearance of disorder; yet we feel peaceful there."

— Natalie Goldberg

Our grief is not orderly. Oh sure, we try keep it in check. We try to make it just so—allowing ourselves a little hug, handshake, or cry now and then but for the most part keeping it on the rails. We've found that if we work really hard, we can corral it.

Our vigilance over our grief is exhausting, though. We're tired of restraint. What happens when we let it run amuck instead?

Paradoxically, when we surrender to grief's unrestraint, we feel a sense of peace. Because like the forest, grief is naturally wild and disorderly. There is tranquility in accepting things as they are.

I will accept my grief as the wild and disorderly experience it is. In acceptance lies peace.

FEBRUARY 2

"What would you do if you were stuck in one place and every day was exactly the same, and nothing that you did mattered?"
— Phil, in the movie *Groundhog Day*

In case you haven't seen it, the romantic comedy movie *Groundhog Day* is about a jaded, self-centered man who has to live the same exact day over and over again. Our grief can feel like that, I've noticed. We wake up to the same horrible realization every day, and while the inconsequential particulars of each day may vary, we have no choice but to slog through another 24 hours of pain and despair.

We're stuck in one place. Every day seems the same. Nothing we do matters.

In the film, the main character, Phil, eventually starts trying different things in an effort to enjoy his endless Groundhog Day. He learns to play the piano, sculpt ice, speak French, and most of all, make friends and help others. Only when he learns to focus on love and connection with others is the time loop broken. Huh. Whaddya know.

When I feel stuck in my grief, I will make an effort to connect with others. This will help me get unstuck.

FEBRUARY 3

"Every great loss demands that we choose life again. We need to grieve in order to do this. The pain we have not grieved over will always stand between us and life. When we don't grieve, a part of us becomes caught in the past like Lot's wife who, because she looked back, was turned into a pillar of salt. Grieving is not about forgetting. Grieving allows us to heal, to remember with love rather than pain. It is a sorting process. One by one you let go of the things that are gone and you mourn for them. One by one you take hold of the things that have become a part of who you are and build again."

— Rachel Naomi Remen

Mourning is the process of choosing life again. When we acknowledge our grief then embrace and express it, we are choosing to engage. And choosing to engage is choosing to live.

I don't know about you, but I want to live. Even though my heart has been broken by loss many times, I find ways to mend it so that I can go on living. It's a scarred, patched-up, cobbled-together heart by now, but it's also bigger and stronger than it was when I got started.

Our human lives are privileges. Mourning affirms this.

I don't want to turn into a pillar of salt. I want to live. Truly live. And so I will remember, grieve, mourn, and build again.

FEBRUARY 4

"Don't cry because it's over. Smile because it happened."
— Dr. Seuss

Mostly I love Dr. Seuss, but here he perpetuates one of our culture's most predominant misconceptions about grief: We shouldn't be sad because…

- the people who died wouldn't want us to be sad.

- crying doesn't do anyone any good.

- we deserve to be happy.

But we ARE sad! Of course we are! And if we ARE sad, that means we *need* to be sad.

What's more, crying is great for our bodies and souls because it releases stress chemicals, signals to others we need support, and helps us feel better afterward. It's a form of active mourning, and active mourning is always good.

When you run into this quote by Dr. Seuss (and you will; it's everywhere), here's what I want you to think to yourself instead: Cry because it's over AND smile because it happened. Crying is good for us. So is learning to smile at the good memories and the love we still feel. The two actions are not mutually exclusive; they go hand-in-hand.

I can cry because it's over and also smile because it happened.

FEBRUARY 5

"When someone you love becomes a memory,
that memory becomes a treasure."
— Author Unknown

One of our essential needs of mourning is to remember the person who died. At first it is often painful to remember, but over time, remembering usually becomes easier and more rewarding.

When we're ready, undertaking projects of memory-gathering and –preserving can help us heal our grief. Putting together a special photo album or scrapbook of the person who died is one example. Making a memory box filled with not only photos but also mementos and souvenirs is another.

If we're feeling inspired, we can also gather up the memories of others by asking them to email us anecdotes or thoughts about our special person. Or we can do informal interviews, jotting down the memories of others as they speak them to us. We can even piece together a biography of sorts—a single document that tries to capture as much as possible about the life of the person who died. If we want, we can publish this document in book-form using simple online tools.

Our memories are indeed treasures. Memory-gathering and -preserving activities treat our treasures with the honor and respect they deserve. They also allow us to pass on our treasures to future generations.

If I want to gather and preserve memories,
I can do it in ways that feel right to me.
I may also ask others to help me with these projects.

FEBRUARY 6

*"The meaning of life. The wasted years of life. The poor choices of life.
God answers the mess of life with one word: 'grace.'"*
— Max Lucado

When we are grieving, our lives often seem messy, chaotic,
even pointless. We are confused. We are disorganized and
disconnected. We are casting about for something solid
to hold onto and finding nothing. Help!

And then along comes grace.

Grace is the experience of synchronicity and blessings in life. It
is the recognition that this moment is good, even magical. In the
midst of our turmoil, we receive a hug from a child. Or we look
up and marvel at the clouds overhead. Or we see what we
know is a sign from our loved one who died.

Grace is ours for the embracing. It is available to us every
day if we only open wide our hearts.

*Grace, I will be on the watch for you
and be thankful whenever you appear.*

FEBRUARY 7

"Some things don't matter much. Like the color of a house. How big is that in the overall scheme of life? But lifting a person's heart—now, that matters. The whole problem with people is…they know what matters, but they don't choose it… The hardest thing on earth is choosing what matters."

— Sue Monk Kidd

We tend to go through the routines of our days without spending much time on the things that matter most to us. But when we lose someone we love, we become acutely aware of what really matters versus what we're doing with our days.

Why are we not spending more time with the people we love? Why are we working so hard? Why are we fussing about our furniture or our cars or the color of our house?
Death is a great clarifier.

The hardest thing on earth is choosing what matters. Now that we've been forced into a situation where we can viscerally see, feel, and understand what really matters, shouldn't we start choosing it?

As much as possible, I will choose to spend today (and the remainder of my todays) on what really matters.

FEBRUARY 8

"For some moments in life there are no words."
– David Seltzer

We find that we cannot always talk about our grief. It is bigger than words. It is wider than words. It is so much deeper and more profound than words.

When language fails us, we can turn to other forms of expression. We might find comfort in hugs and holding hands. We may be helped by creating artwork, playing or listening to music, or participating in some form of physical activity. Rituals such as lighting candles and attending spiritual services also transcend language and give our grief a healing outlet.

When I am unable or unwilling to express my grief in conversation, I will find other ways to share it.

FEBRUARY 9

"Trust yourself. You've survived a lot,
and you'll survive whatever is coming."
— Robert Tew

People we've loved with all our hearts have died…and yet,
here we are. We have survived.

In the beginning, it didn't seem like we'd be able to survive. The
reality was too terrible. The pain was too crushing.
We were sure it would kill us.

But we lived. We live. Maybe now we can trust in ourselves to
live through whatever is coming. Maybe now we can trust that
even when all hope seems lost, things will get better.

I am learning to trust that I instinctively know what
I need to survive, grieve, mourn, and heal.

FEBRUARY 10

"Mountains cannot be surmounted except by winding paths."
— Von Goethe

I live in the foothills of the Rocky Mountains and enjoy hiking on the many spectacular trails. But when I set off on a challenging hike, knowing that I'm going to climb 1,000 vertical feet over the next four or five miles, it is a daunting prospect. That's a thousand stair-steps!

That's where the switchbacks come in. The trail doesn't take me straight up the mountain. Instead, it meanders back and forth, up and around and down a bit then up and around some more. It spreads out the hardest parts, allowing me to recover on the relatively flattish bits in between. I can also—and do— stop to rest many times along the way.

Our grief is also an uphill climb accomplished on winding paths. The switchbacks can make the journey seem endless, and we may sometimes feel lost, but it's the back-and-forth that makes the trek doable. And we can—and should— stop often to take rests along the way.

When I feel lost in my grief, I'll think of the winding path and trust that I am not lost—I'm simply meandering back and forth as I climb. I'll also stop to take rests as often as I need to.

FEBRUARY 11

"A year from now you will wish you had started today."
— Karen Lamb

We grievers can be procrastinators. We're naturally depressed,
and our energy is low, and so we put things off.
And off. And off.

It's normal and even necessary to procrastinate in early grief.
We're sitting in the wound of our grief, thank you very much.
We need to turn inward and focus on our grief right now.
Please understand our need for space. We'll get to
whatever needs doing when we get to it.

The one thing we shouldn't put off for too long is expressing
our grief. Procrastinated mourning turns into carried grief,
which is grief we never express. And carried grief turns
into all kinds of problems in our lives.

That feeling that's been weighing us down? It's time to talk
about it. That idea that is bothering us and keeping us awake
at night? It's time to write about it in our journals or maybe
talk to a spiritual mentor about. A year from now is too late.
When in doubt, let it out.

The time to express my grief thoughts and feelings has arrived.

FEBRUARY 12

"Gratitude unlocks the fullness of life. It turns what we have into enough, and more. It turns denial into acceptance, chaos to order, confusion to clarity. It can turn a meal into a feast, a house into a home, a stranger into a friend. Gratitude makes sense of our past, brings peace for today, and creates a vision for tomorrow."

— Melody Beattie

Oh the gifts of gratitude. When we are grieving, however, it can be hard to find gratitude—especially in the early weeks and months. Someone who gave our life meaning has been taken from us! How can we be grateful?

But gratitude is where our love lives. When we find ways to remember and continue to revel in our love for the person who died, we are feeling grateful for the time we were privileged to share. And when we focus our awareness on the love we feel for others who continue to be present in our lives as well as on the simple pleasures we experience each day, we are grabbing hold of gratitude.

Training ourselves to live in gratitude as much as possible is central to our healing. It takes effort and discipline, but we can do it—and the reward is a renewed life of meaning and joy.

Today I will focus on appreciating all the blessings in my life. When I feel my grief, I will allow myself to feel it while simultaneously looking on the flipside for my gratitude.

FEBRUARY 13

"Where you used to be, there is a hole in the world, which I find myself constantly walking around in the daytime, and falling into at night. I miss you like hell."

— Edna St. Vincent Millay

We're often so busy during the daytime that we find we can set our grief aside. We groom ourselves, work, go to school, make meals, clean up, walk the dog, make phone calls, stop at the store—anything to distract ourselves from the pain.

But then nighttime comes, and we can no longer hide. Oh sure, we try binging on Netflix and playing games on our computer tablets. We might even have a glass of wine or two. Even so, many nights we end up falling into the hole you left behind in our lives.

If we fall into that hole of missingness tonight, we'll try something other than distractions or lying awake. What if we post on an online grief support group that's up and running 24/7? What if we write in a journal? What if we work on organizing photos and mementos of you?

I miss you like hell. Tonight if I fall into the hole you left behind, I'll engage my grief.

FEBRUARY 14

"The most important business of life is love,
or maybe it's the only one."

— Stendhal

Life is made meaningful by love. Those of us who have been
privileged to love and be loved understand this profound
yet exquisitely simple truth.

Death separates us from the physical presence of those we
love, but it does not—it cannot—separate us from the love
itself. We continue to love even as we grieve. We will keep
loving until our last breath—and who knows,
perhaps beyond.

Love endures. And it is love that will continue
to make our life meaningful.

Whenever I feel my grief, I will try to remember
that I am also feeling my love. I will honor the grief
and give thanks for the love.

FEBRUARY 15

"When those you love die, the best you can do is honor their spirit for as long as you live. You make a commitment that you're going to take whatever lesson that person was trying to teach you, and you make it true in your own life... It's a positive way to keep their spirit alive in the world, by keeping it alive in yourself."

— Patrick Swayze

Someone we love has died, and we are alive. Even though we are grieving and in pain, our lives here on earth continue. This is our new and bittersweet truth.

And yet, part of this truth is that we have a wondrous opportunity. That opportunity is to live and love fully from this moment forward. Perhaps the death has made us more aware of the preciousness of our own lives.

We can also choose to live in honor and memory of the person who died. We can look for ways to celebrate their lives, even as we richly live our own. We can finish something that our loved one left unfinished. We can carry on something they felt passionate about. We can, in essence, try to live for both us.

I will strive to live in ways that honor the person who died as well as the preciousness of life itself.

FEBRUARY 16

"One doesn't discover new lands without consenting to lose sight,
for a very long time, of the shore."
— André Gide

At times our grief is like a beginner's trapeze. We swing back and forth, back and forth. But to really move on to new ways of thinking and feeling, we've got to let go of the trapeze bar we're so desperately clinging to and grab hold of the new one.

In other words, we've got to decide to let go of the familiar. We've got to try new mourning activities. We've got to talk to different people. We've got to muster the courage to set sail and lose sight of the shore.

What's the worst that could happen? We could get lost—but we're already lost, aren't we? More likely we'll encounter new sights and sensations, new ways of thinking, and in discovering new lands, we'll learn to thrive and not just survive.

I'm ready to lose sight of the shore. Bon voyage!

FEBRUARY 17

"To embrace one's brokenness, whatever it looks like, whatever has caused it, carries within it the possibility that one might come to embrace one's healing."

— Robert Benson

Embracing our brokenness may be the most difficult thing we will ever do in this life. Embracing love and joy—yes, please! More, more, more! But embracing pain, sadness, despair, disappointment, and regret—no, thanks!

Yet what choice do we have? We're *feeling* the pain, sadness, despair, disappointment, and regret. If we ignore or try to deny these feelings, they won't go away. Not really. They'll destroy the remainder of our lives through problems like depression, anxiety, and relationship troubles.

So we muster the courage to embrace our pain, and in doing so, we embrace our eventual healing.

My brokenness hurts, but befriending it means befriending my eventual healing. So here I go.

FEBRUARY 18

*"What I like best about cell phones is that I can talk to myself
in the car now and nobody thinks it's weird."*

— Ron Brackin

Lots of mourners I've known find it healing to talk out loud to
the person who died. They imagine that he's somewhere they
can't see him—near or far—but that he can hear every
word they say and is always listening.

We can talk to photos of the person who died. We can make
it part of our daily routines to say "Good morning!" and
"Goodnight!" to that photo on our nightstand. We can visit the
cemetery, columbarium, or scattering site and talk out loud.
We can use the time we spend in our cars talking
to the person who died.

Talking out loud to the person who died is a form of
mourning because it's expressing our thoughts and feelings
outside of ourselves. It's also a way for us to continue our
relationship of love with our special person. And who
knows…maybe they actually *can* hear us!

*Any time I feel like talking to you, I can talk to you.
The more I do it, the more natural and helpful it becomes.*

FEBRUARY 19

"No one ever told me grief felt so like fear."
— C.S. Lewis

Feelings of anxiety, panic, and fear are often part of our grief experience. Our sense of security has been threatened, so we are naturally anxious. We find ourselves wondering, "Am I going to be OK? Will I survive this? What might happen next?"

We may be afraid of what the future holds or that we will experience other losses. We may be more aware of our own vulnerability or mortality, which can be scary.

We may feel panicky about our inability to concentrate. Financial problems can compound our feelings of anxiety.

Essentially, all is not well in our worlds, which can make us feel anxious and afraid. Talking our fears through with someone who cares about us and can listen without simply telling us we don't need to be afraid is a way through. Working on self-calming techniques and rituals is another.

I will notice what calms me down when I feel afraid or anxious. I will turn to these healthy self-calming techniques whenever I need to. I will also speak my fears aloud to a good listener.

FEBRUARY 20

I've developed a new philosophy. I only dread one day at a time."
— Charlie Brown (Charles M. Schulz)

Dread is the feeling of debilitating worry about something. It's the expectation that an upcoming experience is going to be terrible.

In grief, it's normal to dread certain things. We might dread the anniversary of the death or the next holiday. We might dread going through our loved one's things or sorting photos. More generally, we might dread the coming weeks and months because we expect them to be so very painful.

While it's normal to feel dread, it's also within our power to change our expectations. After all, expectations aren't reality. They're our projection of what reality is *going* to be like. They're the story we're telling ourselves about what will happen. And have you ever noticed that things rarely turn out as badly as we expect them to?

So…maybe we can sometimes choose to expect more pleasant outcomes instead.

When I'm dreading something, I can choose to tell myself
a more pleasant story of expectation instead.

FEBRUARY 21

"Everyone grieves in different ways. For some, it could take longer or shorter. I do know it never disappears. An ember still smolders inside me. Most days, I don't notice it, but, out of the blue, it'll flare to life."
— Maria V. Snyder

We grievers are all susceptible to griefbursts. Even long, long after the death, something as simple as a smell, a word, a gesture, or a memory can bring our loss crashing back upon us. We gasp at the pain and may find ourselves sobbing. The experience brings us to our knees.

Griefbursts may be draining, but they are also normal and natural. They are proof that our grief always lives inside us, and when something touches that grief—it flares to life.

We can't prevent griefbursts, but we can learn to embrace them when they flare up. They simply let us know that our grief still needs our attention now and then.

The next time I experience a griefburst, I will stop what I'm doing and give it my full attention until it softens.

FEBRUARY 22

"I wanted to talk to someone. But who? It's moments like this, when you need someone the most, that your world seems smallest."

— Rachel Cohn

For some of us, the person who died was our closest ally and best listener. Now we need to talk to someone about our grief…but the someone we need most is…gone. Others of us have many acquaintances but lack close confidants.

So whom do we talk to? We're faced with nurturing closer bonds with other people in our lives, or finding new friends. Both can seem like daunting tasks.

If we know someone who's naturally empathetic and a skilled listener, we can start there. We can try a counselor or support group. Someone who has experienced a similar loss is also a good possibility.

When we need someone but no one's there, our worlds feel too small. We can break through the smallness by reaching out beyond our usual confines.

I can break through the smallness of my world to connect with others who will listen.

FEBRUARY 23

"Courage doesn't always roar. Sometimes courage is the little voice at the end of the day that says, 'I'll try again tomorrow.'"
— Mary Anne Radmacher

Remember the story about the lion crippled by a thorn stuck in his paw? He roared for help from his fellow creatures of the African plains, but only the tiny mouse was brave enough to approach and pull the thorn out.

Lots of days our courage in grief is a tiny mouse. It seems small and weak, but if we call upon it, it can still take on little mourning tasks that have great power.

And yes, some days the tiny mouse that is our courage in grief won't emerge at all. When that happens, it's OK to embrace our temporary cowardice (which may simply be a legitimate need to remain inwardly focused) and try again tomorrow.

I believe that little squeaks of courage can do big things. My courage to actively mourn may be small and sometimes not emerge at all, but over time, regular, small actions create life-changing momentum.

FEBRUARY 24

"And I felt like my heart had been so thoroughly and irreparably broken that there could be no real joy again, that at best there might eventually be a little contentment. Everyone wanted me to get help and rejoin life, pick up the pieces and move on, and I tried to, I wanted to, but I just had to lie in the mud with my arms wrapped around myself, eyes closed, grieving, until I didn't have to anymore."

— Anne Lamott

The mud days of our grief are powerful and painful. But there's no going around them. There's only surrendering to the pull of the mud and wallowing.

Lots of people have been contaminated by our culture's avoidance of grief. These are the people who tell us to rejoin life, pick up the pieces, and move on. What they don't realize is they're offering bad advice.

When we feel like lying in the mud with our arms wrapped around ourselves, that means it's time to lie in the mud with our arms wrapped around ourselves. We'll lie there until we don't have to anymore.

If I'm still in the mud days, I'm still in the mud days.
If my mud days have been going on for months on end,
it's time for me to see a grief counselor.
Otherwise, I'm wallowing because I still need to wallow.

FEBRUARY 25

"It's the great mystery of human life that old grief passes gradually into quiet, tender joy."
— Fyodor Dostoyevsky

Over time, our grief softens, but only if we find ways to actively explore and express it. The more we explore and express it, the quieter it becomes.

Eventually we find that our old, well-mourned griefs transform into tender, bittersweet joys. The pain never goes away completely but often takes on the burnished patina of vintage brass.

Human life harbors many mysteries.
Grief is one of the greatest.

The more I explore and express my grief,
with the passage of time
I will find it transforming into bittersweet joy.

FEBRUARY 26

*"Deposits of unfinished grief reside in more American hearts than
I ever imagined. Until these pockets are opened and their contents
aired openly, they block unimagined amounts of human growth and
potential. They can give rise to bizarre and unexplained behavior,
which causes untold internal stress."*

— Robert Kavanaugh

Whenever we lose something or someone important to us,
we grieve inside. But sometimes we do not express our grief.
Instead of mourning, we carry our grief inside us. We try
to wall it in and hope it will heal on its own.

The trouble is, grief unexpressed does not heal on its own.
Time alone does not heal all wounds. And as we accumulate
more loss and unmourned grief, we often find ourselves having
trouble with anxiety, depression, relationships, substance abuse,
and other issues. Uncovering and expressing all our unmourned
griefs leads to profound healing and wellness.

*If I am struggling, I will look to my past for unmourned grief.
I will find a compassionate counselor to help me explore,
express, and finally heal.*

FEBRUARY 27

"When you do nothing, you feel overwhelmed and powerless. But when you get involved, you feel the sense of hope and accomplishment that comes from knowing you are working to make things better."

— Pauline R. Kezer

Many people do little or nothing with their grief. Buying into the cultural misconception that it's better to keep their grief to themselves and "get over it" as quickly as possible, they lock their true thoughts and feelings inside and end up feeling overwhelmed and powerless.

But when we get involved with our grief, when we put it in motion through mourning, we feel hopeful. We feel that sense of accomplishment that comes from knowing we are working to make things better for ourselves.

That's the sad thing about our culture's grief avoidance. It actually hurts us. Only by engaging with our grief do we heal.

Today I will get involved with my grief.

FEBRUARY 28

*"Walking with a friend in the dark is better than
walking alone in the light."*

— Helen Keller

In the darkness of our grief, true friends can be hard to come
by. It's tough spending time with people in mourning. But if we
make an effort to connect with someone who has experienced a
similar loss, we may find just the support we need right now.

A "grief buddy" is a friend—maybe a new friend—with whom
we share a bond of grief. I often call such people our fellow
travelers. They too are journeying through the wilderness of
grief and would often appreciate some company.

Grief buddies can meet for coffee, lunch, a walk, or a golf game.
Any activity that allows us to regularly spend time talking
together will work. The mutual understanding we can
provide one another feels like such a relief.

*I'll think about this grief buddy idea today, and I'll take steps
toward connecting with someone.*

MARCH 1

*"Life is amazing. And then it's awful. And then it's amazing again.
And in between the amazing and the awful it's ordinary and
mundane and routine. Breathe in the amazing, hold on through the
awful, and relax and exhale during the ordinary. That's just living
heartbreaking, soul-healing, amazing, awful, ordinary life.
And it's breathtakingly beautiful."*

— L.R. Knost

Grief can be awful. Life can be awful in grief.

The word "awful" originally came from *awe + full*. Full of awe.
"Awe" is like wonder, except not as happy. The psychologist
Robert Plutchik said awe is a combination of fear and surprise.
Huh. I guess our grief can be surprisingly fearful.
Fearfully surprising, too.

If we regard our grief with awe instead of disdain, if we respect
it instead of trying to ignore it, we're giving it its due. It's hard to
hold on through the awful, but it's also unavoidable. And with
time and effort, that holding on will bring us
round to amazing again.

**I know that life is both amazing and awful. My privilege
at one requires my presence at the other.**

MARCH 2

"The root of all health is in the brain. The trunk of it is in emotion. The branches and leaves are the body. The flower of health blooms when all parts work together."

— Kurdish Saying

Our grief affects our bodies. We often feel tired, achy, and run down. We might catch viruses more easily, and physical problems we had before the death might get worse.

Sometimes we also seem to be feeling the physical symptoms of the person who died. If she died of a brain tumor, for example, we might notice we are having headaches. If he died from a heart attack, we might feel chest pain. While it's important to see a doctor to make sure, what's usually happening is that our bodies are trying to identify with and remain close to the person who died.

Don't be shocked if you experience physical symptoms that relate somehow to the person who died. You're not crazy. Your body is simply responding to the loss. As you heal your heart and soul, which I believe are the true root of all health, your body will start to feel better.

My body is grieving, too, and deserves gentle care. It misses the person who died.

MARCH 3

"God, grant me the serenity to accept the things I cannot change,
The courage to change the things I can,
And the wisdom to know the difference."

— Reinhold Niebuhr *(Serenity Prayer)*

In the storm of our grief, serenity often eludes us. We may feel anything but at peace. We may be anxious or afraid. We may feel chaotic, depressed, or regretful. The winds howl and the rains batter us. The thunder and lightning keep us on edge.

We yearn for the calm of serenity, and therein lies the paradox.

It is in accepting the storm of our grief—which we cannot change—that we move toward serenity. It is in finding the courage to fully experience the storm that we eventually change it.

God grant me the courage and wisdom to embrace my grief so that I can move toward serenity.

MARCH 4

*"Her grief was so big and wild it terrified her, like an evil beast
that had erupted from under the floorboards."*

— J.K. Rowling

Sometimes our own grief scares us. It can be violent, wracking,
and loud. It can scream, wail, and keen. It can be erratic and
out of control. Even among those of us who are normally quiet,
buttoned-up people, our grief can now and then explode.

Let's think of it this way: Our grief is as big and powerful as our
love was. When someone who made our life worth living is
taken away from us, of course our grief goes crazy with rage and
fear and despair! It's like a dragon guarding its treasure.
Oh, the wrath when the treasure is stolen!

The next time our grief terrifies us, we can remember our
dragons. Something precious has been stolen from them.
They've been awoken. It's only normal and natural
for them to roar in protest.

*My grief is big and wild. When it needs to erupt,
it's OK to let it erupt.*

MARCH 5

"A friend who can be silent with us in a moment of confusion or despair, who can stay with us in an hour of grief and bereavement, who can tolerate not knowing…not healing…not curing… that is a friend indeed."

— Henri Nouwen

On our journey through grief, we need companions who can walk alongside us. Who can listen to us talk without feeling the need to give us solutions. Who can be present to our pain without trying to distract us or immediately soothe it away. Who can bear witness to the truth of our mourning.

We all know people who are not good friends in grief. Some are not able to sit with us in our pain. They neither help nor hinder us.

Others, with their judging or their toxic attitudes, can be downright harmful to us.

We will instead seek out the compassionate helpers who can stay with us in our hour of grief and hold our hand.

If I give it thought, I can identify at least one person who could be a good friend to me in grief. I will reach out to that person and accept her companionship.

MARCH 6

"The thought of suicide is a great consolation:
by means of it one gets through many a dark night."
— Friedrich Nietzsche

Sometimes the pain of our grief is so overwhelming that we
wish it could just all be over. We wouldn't mind, we think,
if we just didn't wake up tomorrow.

Such passive and passing suicidal thoughts in grief are natural.
They can be a consolation. What's *not* natural is actively wanting
to or making plans to take your own life.

If you have been thinking about taking your own life, please,
talk to a professional helper right away. Sometimes the tunnel
vision of grief can prevent you from seeing choices. You can and
will start to feel better, and seeing a counselor or calling a
crisis hotline is a step toward healing.

If my thoughts of suicide take on planning and structure,
that means it's time for me to get help.

MARCH 7

*"If you aren't sure who you are, you might as well work
on who you want to be."*
— Robert Brault

One of the most challenging needs we have in grief is that of
creating a new self-identity. We're different now. We might have
gone from being a spouse to a widow or widower,
for example, or a child to an orphan.

Other changes we are undergoing don't have simple labels. We
feel shaken to the core, and every rope that tethered us to our
sense of how the world works has been cut or at least frayed.

As we work to re-anchor ourselves, we may discover some
positive aspects of our changing self-identities. We may be
more confident than we were before, for example, or more
compassionate. We can also take advantage of this forced
reconstruction time by working on who we most
want to be from here on out.

*I'm not sure who I am anymore.
It will take time and hard work to figure it out.*

MARCH 8

"There are times we must sink to the bottom of our misery to understand truth, just as we must descend to the bottom of a well to see the stars in broad daylight."

— Vaclav Havel

We're sinking. We're descending. We feel as if our grief is pulling us under…down, down, down.

It's not easy to sink. We might fight it. We might flail about, resisting the need to acknowledge the reality of what happened and descend into the pain.

But if we learn to surrender and relax into our misery, the journey gets a bit easier. We are less fatigued and more at peace. And we begin to understand the truth that we must descend before we can transcend. Down we go.

The bonus? At the bottom, we will discover that we can better see the stars.

I am sinking. I can relax and allow myself to sink, trusting I will touch bottom and rise again.

MARCH 9

"Cynicism masquerades as wisdom, but it is the furthest thing from it. Because cynics don't learn anything. Because cynicism is self-imposed blindness: a rejection of the world because we are afraid it will hurt us or disappoint us. Cynics always say 'no.' But saying 'yes' begins things. Saying 'yes' is how things grow."

— Stephen Colbert

We grievers have earned a little cynicism. After all, life has hurt us. We engaged with life, and in the end it dealt us a mean blow.

We're probably going to say 'no' for a while. We're going to crawl into our shells and regroup. We won't re-engage quickly or easily.

But soon there will come a time when we need to start saying 'yes' again. 'Yes' to our friends and family. 'Yes' to new experiences. 'Yes' to love and life. 'Yes' begins things. 'Yes' is how things grow.

Living a life of 'no' is no life at all.

As soon as I'm ready, I will start looking for opportunities to say 'yes.'

MARCH 10

"God, why do I storm heaven for answers that are already in my heart? Every grace I need has already been given me. Oh, lead me to the Beyond within."

— Macrina Wiederkehr

One of the most surprising things about grief is that it is really a process of getting to know ourselves. We were blithely living our lives, not giving much thought to what we were doing and why, when death pulled back the curtain.

Suddenly we're asking the Big Questions that we didn't pay attention to before. And we're finding that the answers— to the extent there *are* answers—lie within us.

God built us to love, which means God also built us to grieve. He entrusted us with the Big Questions and the search for answers.

Every grace we need has already been given us. We just need to look within.

Every grace I need has already been given me. Oh, lead me to the Beyond within.

MARCH 11

"A wound does not destroy us. It activates our self-healing powers.
The point is not to 'put it behind you' but to keep benefiting
from the strength it has awakened."

— David Richo

Early in our grief, it feels like our loss might destroy us. But as
we learn to trust in the healing powers of active mourning, we
realize that not only can we survive, we can go on to thrive.

It takes courage and strength to mourn openly, honestly, and
fully. But once we unleash that strength—watch out.
We are a force to be reckoned with.

We no longer tolerate pettiness or meanness. We know what
matters, and by God, we're not going to put up with any
more nonsense. We are not putting our loss behind us. As the
Japanese author Kenji Miyazawa said, we are going to
burn it as fuel for our journey forward.

I am stronger now than I was before. May I find ways to benefit
from my newfound strength and to help others benefit as well.

MARCH 12

"Never go to bed mad. Stay up and fight."
— Phyllis Diller

Now that's a joke that contains surprising wisdom.

In grief, we can translate it to: If we're feeling a strong feeling or thinking a dominant thought, we should express it before we go to bed. If we don't, what will happen? We'll likely lie there ruminating and stressing, unable to fall asleep.
And we need sleep to function and heal!

Here are some ways we can release our nighttime thoughts and feelings: text a friend, write in a journal we keep in our nightstands, talk to our partner or someone who lives with us, hop online and do some sharing on a grief forum, post on social media, meditate, or pray.

Let's not turn out the lights on our pent-up thoughts and feelings. Let's let them out so they can run around a bit while we get some much-needed sleep.

Tonight I'll make an effort to share any thoughts and feelings that are weighing on my heart and mind before I turn out the lights.

MARCH 13

"Never, ever underestimate the importance of having fun."
— Randy Pausch

Fun and grief can seem like oil and water.
They just don't go together.

But they're really more like oil and vinegar. Add a little mustard
or egg yolk, and they can be blended. And together they
create an emulsion that makes our grief survivable.

Randy Pausch was the 48-year-old Carnegie Mellon professor
who, upon learning he had terminal pancreatic cancer, gave a
lecture and wrote a bestselling book called *The Last Lecture*. In
them he imparted his newfound understanding
of what really matters in life.

So when a man with only months to live tells us to never, ever
underestimate the importance of having fun, let's do as he says.

*I need to make a point of having fun now
and then while I'm grieving.*

MARCH 14

*"You are unrepeatable. There is a magic about you
that is all your own."*

— D.M. Dellinger

Our grief makes us aware of our dependence on others, for it is
our relationships, when severed, that give rise to our grief.

Loving and being loved is the reason for life, yet at the same
time, you, all by yourself, embody unique talents and gifts. You
are unrepeatable. I am unrepeatable. There is a magic
about us that is all our own.

Cultivating our gifts and sharing them with the world is the
other reason for life, I believe. We were born to love and be
loved, yes, but also to use our unique gifts to help others.

As we mourn, we can also, when we are ready, leverage our
abilities to make a difference. In doing so, we are opening our
hearts to new people and relationships. We are expressing
ourselves in ways that form more connections. We are enriching
our own lives as well as the lives of others.

*There is a magic about me. I will find ways to
own this magic and share it with others.*

MARCH 15

"Beware the Ides of March."
— William Shakespeare

The "Ides of March" is March 15th. In Shakespeare's play *Julius Caesar*, the soothsayer says to Julius, "Beware the Ides of March," warning him of his impending death. Ever since, March 15th has been a date associated with foreboding and death.

We can use this day to give some thought to our own eventual deaths. How would we hope to be remembered? What tasks would we like to have finished? How will our friends and family talk about us long after our funerals?

Our loss wakes us up to the fleetingness of life. Now that we're awake, shouldn't we take steps to start—this very day!—being who we most want to be and doing what we most want to do?

I have hopes and dreams to fulfill before I die.
Today I take action.

MARCH 16

"When someone you love dies, and you're not expecting it, you don't lose her all at once; you lose her in pieces over a long time—the way the mail stops coming, and her scent fades from the pillows and even from the clothes in her closet and drawers. Gradually, you accumulate the parts of her that are gone. Just when the day comes— when there's a particular missing part that overwhelms you with the feeling that she's gone, forever—there comes another day, and another specifically missing part."

— John Irving

Grief is a one day-at-a-time thing. That's why we're working through this book together. And part of its day-to-day nature has to do with the new facets of loss that confront us so often.

Yesterday it was picking up her hairbrush and touching the strands tangled there. The day before that it was the realization that he won't be here for our birthday this year. Last week it was coming across a note she wrote long ago. And tomorrow? Who knows what fresh reminders of our loss tomorrow holds?

It's hard, this accumulating of your absence. But maybe you're just trying to remind us that you're still around after all.

I'm losing you in pieces. I'm holding on to you in pieces too.

MARCH 17

"Many an opportunity is lost because a man
is out looking for four-leaf clovers."
— Author Unknown

Sometimes we fall prey to the thinking that what we have isn't good enough. We need a bigger TV, a nicer car, and a better vacation—and then we'll be happy. In grief, we're also focusing on what we lack. This time, at least, the lack is something truly important—the physical presence of someone we love. But what about the friends and family members who are still here?

You'll have noticed by now that I'm a big advocate for grieving and mourning. We *do* need to grieve after someone we love dies, and we *do* need to express our grief. We *do* need to focus on the lack. It's disingenuous to think we can simply "look on the bright side" or "count our blessings."

And yet, while we're grieving, we can also learn to see each day as an opportunity to live and love fully. If we are alive and we love and are loved, that is opportunity plenty.

My life is not a perfect four-leaf clover, but it is still beautiful.

MARCH 18

"The first time someone shows you who they are, believe them."
— Maya Angelou

Not everyone is cut out to be a good friend in grief. You've probably learned this already. People you would have expected to support you fall out of touch, while others you never imagined would support you do.

One way to respond in the face of faltering friendships is to be proactive and honest. Even though we're the ones who are grieving, we may need to be the ones to phone our friends and keep in touch. When we do speak, let's be honest. Let's tell our friends how we're really and truly feeling and that we appreciate their support. When we find that certain friends can't handle our "grief talk," we can stick to lighter topics with them and lean more heavily on the friends who can support us in our grief.

Some friends will fall away permanently; others will step away for a time then return. That is life. We are all fluid beings who never stop becoming. Knowing this, we can respond with grace.

No matter how others respond to my grief, I can offer them my Namaste: The divine in me honors the divine in you.

MARCH 19

"Grief is the last act of love we have to give to those we loved.
Where there is deep grief, there was great love."
— Author Unknown

Grief is the flipside of love. When those we love leave us behind, we go on loving, but now the love is made bittersweet by the fact that they are no longer physically here to receive it.

What if we think of our grief as an act of love? After all, that's really what it is. Does that change how we feel about it?

If we loved greatly, we will grieve deeply. That's the equation. Let's honor our special people who have died with grief and mourning that is as wide and as deep as our love for them still is.

I loved greatly, and now I grieve deeply.
My grief is an act of love.

MARCH 20

"I may try to protect myself from my sadness by not talking about my loss. I may even secretly hope that the person who died will come back if I don't talk about it. Yet, as difficult as it is, I must feel it to heal it."

— Alan Wolfelt

Death is often the elephant in the room. It's big. It's there, hulking in the corner. But we go on blithely with our lives, pretending it's not.

We do this because our culture isn't good at embracing death, loss, and grief as natural parts of life. And so we all pretend. We look away. We stick our fingers in our ears, close our eyes, and refuse to listen and look. Even when our own lives are impacted by a significant death, we sometimes still go on pretending— to others and sometimes even to ourselves.

But life is so much fuller and richer and more genuine when we embrace the elephant! He's such an essential part of human life! We should talk about him just as openly and often as we talk about the "good things." We should befriend the feelings he evokes in us. It is this very honesty that allows us to begin to heal.

I must acknowledge my grief, and I must feel it to heal it.

MARCH 21

"Despite the forecast, live like it's spring."
— Lilly Pulitzer

Depending on the day and our moods, the forecast can seem to call for nonstop cold and wet when we're grieving.

The paradox is that we can learn both to inhabit the dreary days and expect spring at the same time. In other words, we can embrace the pain and darkness of our grief when that is what we are feeling while also nurturing hope that sunshine and flower blossoms are on the way.

Healing in grief is a lot like the onset of spring. It's unreliable and fickle. One day it's warmish and blue skies and we think, "Hey! We're feeling better!" Then the next day—or week—it's sleeting and gray again. But ever so slowly, we advance into better weather. We can't rush it. We can't control it. We can't skip the dismal days. But we can trust that spring and then summer will come.

No matter how I'm feeling today,
I will trust that better days are ahead.

MARCH 22

*"Many of us spend our whole lives running from feeling with the
mistaken belief that you cannot bear the pain. But you have already
borne the pain. What you have not done is feel
all you are beyond that pain."*

— Kahlil Gibran

We're bearing our pain. Even though some days it feels
unbearable, we somehow make it through. Here we are.

So let's not run away from our feelings. We can bear them.
We *are* bearing them. But there's a difference between coping
and embracing. If we're coping, we're just getting by. If we're
embracing, we're turning toward our grief and befriending it.
We're welcoming it with open arms.

Embracing the truth of everything we are thinking and feeling
and then expressing that truth is the most transformative way to
move beyond the pain. We can cope or we can embrace. We can
just get by or we can go all in. We can survive or we can thrive.

*I choose to embrace and express my pain in order to feel
all I am beyond my pain.*

MARCH 23

*"But grief makes a monster out of us sometimes…
and sometimes you say and do things to the people you love
that you can't forgive yourself for."*

— Melina Marchetta

Sometimes mourning has bad manners. We feel rage. We place blame. We yell; we snap; we speak harshly. We can be unkind. Yet anger, hate, blame, terror, resentment, rage, and jealousy are normal and often necessary parts of our grief journeys.
These feelings are essentially a form of protest. Think of the toddler whose favorite toy is yanked out of his hands. When it's taken, his instinctive reaction may be to scream or cry or hit. When someone loved is taken from us, our instinctive reaction may be much the same.

If our explosive emotions hurt others, we can apologize. We can also explain that our grief sometimes makes us behave badly. Sharing this truth will foster forgiveness and healing.

*When grief makes a monster out of me, I will try to find
constructive ways to express my explosive emotions.*

MARCH 24

*"We learn, grow, and become compassionate and generous as much
through exile as homecoming, as much through loss as gain."*

— David Whyte

I'd like to talk a little about the idea of exile today. To be exiled
usually means to be forced away to a distant place. Our grief
certainly exiles us from the life we were living. It sends us away
to a new and harsh land where nothing quite makes
sense and life is lonely and hard.

So there is that sense of exile in grief. But there is also another,
more healing way to think about it. When we retreat to a place
of spiritual contemplation and beauty, we are also going to exile.
The word "contemplate" means to create space for the divine
to enter. So if we exile ourselves to a special place—as simple
as a quiet room we love, as plain as a park or a path in the
forest, as far removed as a visit to a monastery or other spiritual
destination—we are opening our hearts, minds, and souls to
contemplation. We are creating space for the divine to enter.

When we are feeling the dissonance between our grief and the
busy-ness of our daily lives, let's remember to take ourselves to
exile. It is there that we can nurture ourselves, be with our grief,
and do our sacred work of mourning.

I will find ways to go to exile.

MARCH 25

"My grief, I find, is not desolation or rebellion at universal law or deity. I find grief to be much simpler and sadder... All the things he loved tear at my heart because he is no longer here on earth to enjoy them. All the things he loved!"

— John Gunther

All the things you loved, dear one! They're still here, but you are not. Every time we happen upon of these reminders, our hearts are torn apart again. So many days and experiences that for you will never be.

All the things the person who died loved will always prick our hearts. We can choose to act on that pain, though. We can introduce the loved things to someone new. We can volunteer time or give money in support of the things. We can say a silent prayer of gratitude for the things every time we encounter them.

We can also consider finishing something that the person who died left unfinished. What was he most passionate about? Is there something we can do to close a loop or realize a dream?

All the things you loved tear at my heart. Today I'll burn that pain as fuel to carry one of your projects or passions forward.

MARCH 26

"I measure every grief I meet with narrow, probing eyes.
I wonder if it weighs like mine—or has an easier size."
— Emily Dickinson

It's natural to silently compare our losses to those of others. *She's lucky*, we think. *He's had it so much worse*, we shudder.
It's not fair, we judge.

Yet if we remember that grief can't really be weighed and that comparing helps no one, our compassion grows.

Everyone who lives long enough experiences significant losses in life. That is the human condition. And all of our fellow human beings need empathy and support. We do too.

The next time I catch myself comparing griefs, I will remember
that a broken heart is a broken heart. I will express compassion,
and I will nurture self-compassion.

MARCH 27

*"Pain reaches the heart with electrical speed, but truth
moves to the heart as slowly as a glacier."*
— Barbara Kingsolver

It's true. We felt the pain of our grief from the moment we
learned of the death. Even though shock and numbness
protected us from the full force of the hurt in the early days
and weeks, we still felt pain with electrical speed.

It's taking us much longer to sort out the truth about what all of
this means. Why did this person have to die? Why are we here?
What do we have to live for now?

As we naturally search for meaning and give expression to our
wondering, truth begins to move to our hearts. We develop
new understandings and revise our reasons to go on not only
living, but thriving. This process is glacially slow, yet it is also
powerful. The truth, as the Bible says, will set us free.

My truth is slowly making its way to my heart.

MARCH 28

"I hate feelings. Why does sobriety have to come with feelings?"
— Augusten Burroughs

Our feelings of grief are hard to feel. They hurt. And so we sometimes try to mask or dull them with drugs, alcohol, and other addictive behaviors like sex, gambling, or shopping.

But we're learning that inappropriately or indiscriminately turning to drugs, alcohol, or addictive pleasures only brings temporary relief. The hurt is still there, waiting to be felt and embraced.

If you're in over your head with drugs, alcohol, or other addictive behaviors, today's the day to ask for help. Healing both your grief and your unhealthy behaviors is the way to a life of meaning and joy. Don't settle for the hazy shadow life of addiction.

If there's even a tiny chance that I may be slipping into addiction, today's the day I will take a step toward getting help.

MARCH 29

"Blessed are those who mourn: for they shall be comforted."
— Matthew 5:4

When we mourn, which means to express our grief outside
of ourselves, we alert others to our inner pain. We make the
invisible visible. We wear our hearts on our sleeves.
We reach out.

In reaching out to others, we admit that we need help. If we
are used to self-reliance, this admission takes courage. But the
reward for our admission is empathy. Not everyone is equipped
to be a good helper in grief, but those who are give us comfort.
They provide us with the balm of companionship. They bear
witness to our truth and extend the promise of hope.

Of course, we may also be profoundly comforted by our faith,
whatever that uniquely means to us. Faith can be
the most assuaging comfort of all.

I will seek out and welcome healthy comforts in all forms.

MARCH 30

"To share your weakness is to make yourself vulnerable;
to make yourself vulnerable is to show your strength."
— Criss Jami

In the aftermath of our loss, others may tell us to "be strong."
There's no denying that it takes strength and fortitude
to embrace and survive our grief.

But the reverse is even truer. We must allow
ourselves to be weak.

Grief shatters us. It tears us apart. We are tender and weak. And
when we are genuine with others, expressing our most painful
thoughts and feelings, we allow them to see our weakness. We
expose our vulnerable insides. The paradox is that it
takes courage to let others see our weakness.

From our weakness and vulnerability grow our healing.
They are fertile soil.

I will allow myself to be weak and vulnerable. In grief,
weakness is strength, and vulnerability is powerful.

MARCH 31

"The beauty of the unexpected lies within the surprise
of the momentum, not only at its tipping point,
but also within all the moments waiting."

— Akilnathan Logeswaran

Actively expressing our grief sets it in motion. It creates a sense
of movement and change. When there is enough movement, we
experience "divine momentum," which is the feeling that even
though we are still grieving and torn apart, we are heading
in the right direction. We are on a roll.

That feeling of momentum is, well, momentous. We experience
a rush of hopefulness and purpose. We are
surprised by its power.

When it happens, we can pause and give thanks. We can
celebrate our progress, however small. We can also keep actively
engaging our grief, for like the initial push of a pendulum,
it is this effort that perpetuates the momentum.

I will be alert for divine momentum in my grief journey, and
when I feel it, I will give thanks, celebrate, and keep working.

APRIL 1

"Some people feel the rain. Others just get wet."
— Bob Marley

Our grief is like the showers of April. It washes over us, day after day. It can make everything seem cold and dreary.

Still, our challenge is to really feel the rain of our grief. To observe it. To notice its nuances. To focus on it when it wants our attention. To sit in it and fully experience it.

Some people don't soak in their grief in this way. Instead, they just get wet. They don't observe, notice, focus, and befriend. Many times I have seen such people trying to hurriedly dry off without ever having really felt the rain. The problem is, these people tend to never really feel the sunshine again, either.

I appreciate the rain, and in my appreciation, I know that I will also be able to appreciate the sun when it reappears.

APRIL 2

"What day is it?"
"It's today," squeaked Piglet.
"My favorite day," said Pooh.

— A.A. Milne

As Eckhart Tolle emphasizes, our life only ever takes place in the present. Our grief needs us to remember the past, and wonder and worry about the future, but meanwhile, our life is happening in the now.

One way to get better at mindful, in-the-moment living is by pursuing activities that we lose ourselves in. When we are in the flow or "the zone" of doing things that we love, we are fully present.

We can also work to be fully present to our grief. When thoughts and feelings come up, we think and feel them. We do not rush or suppress them. We allow ourselves to experience them in the fullness of time they require.

Today is a day for being present, come what may.

APRIL 3

"Choose your intention carefully and then practice holding your consciousness to it, so it becomes the guiding light in your life."
— John Roger

When we are grieving, we can choose goals and intentions. For example, we might tell ourselves, "I intend to reach out for help from others" because we know this will help us heal and nurture meaningful connections.

Then, as we are going about our daily lives, we can keep checking back in with our carefully chosen intentions. When we notice ourselves clamming up or withdrawing, we can remind ourselves of our intention to reach out for help. In this way, our intentions can help guide us in our grief.

So let's carefully choose at least one grief intention today and practice holding our consciousnesses to it. It will become the guiding light in our darkness.

In my time of grief, I intend to _____.
Today, I intend to _____.

APRIL 4

"You give yourself permission to grieve by recognizing the need for grieving. Grieving is the natural way of working through the loss of a love. Grieving is not weakness nor absence of faith. Grieving is as natural as crying when you are hurt, sleeping when you are tired, or sneezing when your nose itches. It is nature's way of healing a broken heart."

— Doug Manning

We are often hard on ourselves when we are in grief. We judge ourselves, and we push ourselves. We tell ourselves we need to be strong and carry on. We try to keep doing everything that needs to be done.

What we really need, however, is to be gentle with ourselves. We must give ourselves permission to grieve and mourn, because these tasks are the most important things we have to do right now. Nothing is higher priority than allowing our grief to naturally unfold and expressing whatever comes up.

There is no right way to grieve and mourn, but there is only rightness in grief and mourning.

I give myself permission to grieve as long and as deeply as I need to. I also give myself permission to actively express my grief so that I create momentum for healing.

APRIL 5

"Those who love you are not fooled by mistakes you have made or dark images you hold about yourself. They remember your beauty when you feel ugly; your wholeness when you are broken; your innocence when you feel guilty; and your purpose when you are confused."

— Alan Cohen

Sometimes when we're grieving we feel unlovable. We're grouchy, unkempt, tear-streaked, out of sorts. We're a hot mess. We're not fit for company. All we want to do is hide out where no one can see us.

It's times like this that we need to remember that the people who love us most are not fooled. They love us no matter what, and they also remember the best of us.

The people who love us most can help us find our way back to our new best selves. When they want to help, let's let them in.

The people who love me most love me no matter what.
I will call or visit them today.

APRIL 6

"There is a sacredness in tears. They are not the mark of weakness but of power. They speak more eloquently than ten thousand tongues. They are messengers of overwhelming grief… and unspeakable love."
— Washington Irving

Crying is one way in which we instinctively express our grief. Our tears cleanse our bodies, minds, and spirits. Emotional tears carry out stress hormones and other toxins like a river of relief. Tears also stimulate the release of our feel-good hormones called endorphins, which help us feel better after a good cry.

And so we must give ourselves permission to cry— as often and as much as we need to. If we feel like sobbing or wailing, we must sob or wail. Our bodies know how to mourn.

When I feel tears gathering, I will allow them to spill. My body has healing wisdom.

APRIL 7

"Not all those who wander are lost."
— J.R.R. Tolkien

We are wandering in our grief. We are going this way and that, sometimes forward, sometimes backward, sometimes in circles or zigzags. In our wandering, we can feel aimless, even hopeless. We can feel disorganized and disoriented.
We can feel lost.

Grief is indeed a meandering journey—one with no road map.
When we are feeling lost we can remember:
We may be meandering, but we are not lost.
We are doing what we need to do.

When we learn to trust that the wandering will eventually get us where we need to go, it gets easier...and hope reignites.

Grief is all about the journey.
I may be wandering, but I am not lost.

APRIL 8

*"All journeys have secret destinations of which
the traveler is unaware."*
— Martin Buber

We're on this crazy journey we call grief, and we don't even
know where the heck we're going. We don't know where we'll
end up—at least, not exactly. We won't know where
we're going until we get there.

We travelers have two choices, as I see it. We can take the fork
in the road that leads to active mourning and the embracing of
our grief. On that path, we're befriending our pain but we're
also really living and not just surviving. Or we can take the
other path, on which we're denying and avoiding our grief as
much as possible in the hope that we'll get over it that way.

The first path takes us to a renewed, meaningful life; the second
takes us to a dulled, zombie-like existence. The particulars of
both destinations are kept secret from us until we get there. And
so while I don't know exactly what the two versions of
my future life would be like, at the fork in the road
I choose the first path.

*I don't know exactly where I'm going, but I choose
to head toward really living.*

APRIL 9

"Do something today that your future self will thank you for."
- Author Unknown

Here's one of the most important lessons I've learned from not only my own loss experiences but from the thousands of mourners I've worked with over these many years: Our future grieving selves will thank us for actively mourning today.

It's really easy to procrastinate expressing our grief. Tomorrow, we think. Tomorrow I'll: talk to a friend about what's going on / visit the cemetery / write a post on the Facebook page of the person who died / sort through photos / write thank-you notes / look into support groups / et cetera.

But when it comes to moving toward healing in grief, today is almost always better than tomorrow. We don't have to spend our whole day mourning. We just have to do one small thing to move our grief from the inside to the outside. And if we can muster the courage and fortitude to do one small mourning task most days, our future selves will be ecstatic.

Expressing my thoughts and feelings today is something my future self will thank me for.

APRIL 10

"Grieving is like having broken ribs. On the outside you look fine,
but with every breath, it hurts."

— Author Unknown

Our grief doesn't show on our bodies. That leads other people
to think we're fine. I sometimes wish our skin turned purple
when we started grieving. The worse we feel on any given
day, the darker the purple. Grief's invisibility
does no one any favors.

Then, because we live in a culture that tries to hide grief, we
often become complicit with grief's invisibility. "How are you
doing?" people ask us. "Fine," we say. "Pretty well."

I've learned that what "doing well" in grief usually means is
avoiding or hiding it. We're hurting inside, but we're trying to
look and act fine outside. The only remedy is to live our inner
truth by expressing our grief actively and openly. We
tell people our broken hearts hurt like hell.
And in the telling, we begin to heal.

When I'm hurting inside, I'll find ways to show it on the outside.

APRIL 11

"The more you extend kindness to yourself, the more it will become your automatic response to others."
— Wayne Dyer

At no time do we need to be kinder to ourselves than when we are grieving.

Many of us aren't good at self-care, though. So it's a practice we have to recommit to each and every day.

The bonus for our friends, family, and the world at large is that when we're kind to ourselves, we get better at responding with kindness to authors. Kindness is catchy that way.

Today I will be kind to myself. (Repeat every morning.)

APRIL 12

"My entire life can be described in one sentence: It didn't go as planned, and that's OK."
— Rachel Wolchin

You know what they say about the best-laid plans of mice and men: they often go awry.

Wouldn't life be something if we could control its twists and turns? If everyone we loved (including ourselves!) could live in good health and happiness to the ripe old age of, say, 101?

But we can't control our own lives, let alone the lives of others. Things often don't go as planned. That is the reality of human existence. *Qué sera sera.* Surrendering to this truth and embracing its OKness constitutes a large part of our grief work.

My life doesn't always go as planned, and that's OK.

APRIL 13

"April is the cruellest month, breeding
Lilacs out of the dead land, mixing
Memory and desire, stirring
Dull roots with spring rain.
Winter kept us warm, covering
Earth in forgetful snow…"
— T.S. Eliot

Things start to stir in April. While winter enshrouds us in the safety of darkness, stillness, and lethargy, April asks us to get moving. Wake up! Look around you! Life is alive!

Spring's energy can seem cruel when we are grieving. We may find the bursting of new life incongruent with the deadness we still feel inside. We may feel that nature's reawakening is disrespectful or hard to stomach. How can April behave with such frivolity and joy when the people we love are lifeless?

It's OK not to enjoy spring this year. It's OK to rail against the unfairness and cruelty. At the same time, if we are gentle with ourselves, we will heed our hearts and pay attention to our moments of tenderness. When something April touches us, we will give pause and open ourselves to the experience.

I give myself permission to feel how I feel today. When some-thing touches me, I will stop what I am doing and experience it.

APRIL 14

"Life is not a final. It's a series of daily pop quizzes."
— Author Unknown

How will we live out this day?

We are hurting, so it's not going to be a perfect day, or even a good day maybe. But still, the day will confront us with all kinds of unexpected moments—conversations with people, encounters with pets, amazing sights and sounds and tastes and textures, ideas in writing, surprise memories, social media posts, and much more.

If life is a series of daily pop quizzes, then all of the things we will encounter today are on the test. How will we answer?

I can choose to experience this day to the full, including moments of grief.

APRIL 15

"In this world nothing can be said to be certain,
except death and taxes."
— Benjamin Franklin

Certainty is in short supply in this life.

If we open our hearts to others and practice kindness, we will love and be loved. This means we will also grieve. These are certainties. But the hows and the whens and the whys are usually beyond our control.

So let's focus on the certainties. The sun will rise today, and because we loved, we will feel our grief. We will also continue to feel love—for the person who died as well as for the others in our lives we are close to.

In this uncertain life, our love and our grief anchor us.

I am certain that I love and grieve.
These experiences form the core of my existence.

APRIL 16

"People are afraid of themselves, of their own reality—their feelings most of all. People are taught that pain is evil and dangerous. People try to hide their pain. But they're wrong. You feel your strength in the experience of pain. Pain is a feeling. Your feelings are a part of you. If you feel ashamed of them, and hide them, you're letting society destroy your reality. You should stand up for your right to feel your pain."

— Jim Morrison

We have the right to grieve and mourn. We have the right to feel and express our pain. Grief is just as much a part of our reality as is love.

When society encourages us to ignore or quiet our pain (usually because it makes others uncomfortable), we have the right to ignore *them*. We will not let them destroy our right and our need to grieve and mourn.

We are proud that love is our reality. Because love is our reality, grief is now our reality. We will stand up for our right to love and grieve.

I have the right to grieve and mourn. I will not feel ashamed of my need to grieve and mourn.

APRIL 17

*"Trying to forget doesn't work. In fact, it's pretty much
the same as remembering."*
— Rebecca Stead

When someone we love dies, one of our mourning needs is to
remember them. But sometimes we don't *want* to remember. We
wish we could forget. The remembering is just too painful.

But you've probably realized by now that trying to forget
really doesn't work. Keeping busy, distracting ourselves, and
actively stuffing our memories into the closets of our minds—
and locking the door—might work for a while…but those
memories, they're sneaky. They keep creeping back into our
consciousness. They appear in our dreams. Just when we think
we've got them under control, we smell a certain fragrance or
hear a certain piece of music and *whomp*. Our knees
buckle at the power of a memory.

When we learn to embrace our memories, instead—allowing
and even encouraging them then befriending whatever feelings
they evoke—we find that we gain energy by giving up the
pretense of forgetting. We let the power of memory
wash over us and carry us forward.

*I'll invite a memory today, and when it appears,
I'll sit with it and give it the attention it deserves.*

APRIL 18

*"Stories are light. Light is precious in a world so dark.
Begin at the beginning. Make some light."*
— Kate DiCamillo

When we tell the stories of our love and loss, we create
narratives that help us make sense of our lives. This happened
then this happened then this happened. Like the framing
of a house, the structure of our stories gives
them shape and meaning.

Our memories light the structure of our stories.
Light is precious in a world so dark.

Let's tell our stories. Our storytelling transforms us.

Today I will make some light. I will tell my story of love and loss.

APRIL 19

"Better times perhaps await us who are now wretched."
— Virgil

We grievers are wretched. We have been beaten down by the losses of life, and we feel pitiful, sorrowful, and miserable.

But even 2,100 years ago, the ancient Roman poet Virgil understood that things usually get better.
He exhorts us to have hope.

So let us try to nurture hope, even on our most wretched of days. When we are feeling miserable, we can reach out to others who help us feel hopeful, who bear witness to our misery without trying to soothe it away but who also, at the same time, exude optimism.

On my most wretched of days, I will seek out sparks of hope.

APRIL 20

"It's all messy: The hair. The bed. The words. The heart. Life."
— William Leal

Life is messy. Love is messy. And grief is sure as hell messy.

Sometimes the obsessives among us try to clean it up. We try to make everything neat and tidy and orderly. We make up rules, and we try to enforce them. We create boundaries and timelines and schedules.

It doesn't work, though. The natural chaos of our grief is more powerful than any container we try to put it in. It seeps out and Hulks its way wherever it wants to go. So we might as well let it be messy and trust there's meaning in the messiness.

Life is messy. Love is messy. Grief is messy. Messy must be good.

APRIL 21

*"It's no use going back to yesterday, because I was
a different person yesterday."*
— Lewis Carroll

Sometimes we wish we could go back to our yesterdays, but the problem is (other than the currently insurmountable hurdle of time travel), we're not the same people we were yesterday. Our loss has changed us. Our ongoing grief continues to change us.

We're different now. We've learned some things. We've lived through experiences. We're experiencing transformation, which literally means an entire change in form.
There just ain't no goin' back.

We can't return to an old normal. We can only create a new normal. And that, my friends, is a worthy intention.

*I am different than I was before this loss. I am working
to create my new normal.*

APRIL 22

*"Detachment is not that you should own nothing.
But that nothing should own you."*

— Ali ibn abi Talib

Buddhists believe in living a life of detachment, also called non-attachment. While they also believe in loving kindness, they teach us to understand and live with the understanding that everything is ephemeral.

Buddhists strive not to have expectations. They work on relating to the world and what is happening *as it is* rather than *as we wish it could be*. When emotions arise, they teach that we should feel them while also knowing that they will pass.

When we practice detachment in grief, we allow ourselves to think and feel what we are thinking and feeling. We also feel comfortable expressing what we are thinking and feeling. We live our lives having relinquished the illusion of control. We enjoy the good things in the moment but don't concern ourselves with what will happen next. We experience our grief without allowing it to own us.

Today I will live and love and grieve and mourn.

APRIL 23

"My Lord God, I have no idea where I am going. I do not see the road ahead of me. I cannot know for certain where it will end. Nor do I really know myself, and the fact that I think that I am following your will does not mean that I am actually doing so. But I believe that the desire to please you does in fact please you. And I hope I have that desire in all that I am doing. I hope that I will never do anything apart from that desire. And I know that if I do this you will lead me by the right road though I may know nothing about it. Therefore will I trust you always though I may seem to be lost and in the shadow of death. I will not fear, for you are ever with me, and you will never leave me to face my perils alone."

— Thomas Merton

If statistics are to be believed, most—but certainly not all—of us believe in God. For those of us who do, our faith can be a comfort in our grief. We may not know what's ahead, but we work to trust that a force much greater than ourselves is watching out for us.

In this our hour of our need, another way to think about God is as love. Instead of praying to an omnipotent God, we could pray that we will follow and trust in love:

I believe that the desire to love creates love. And I hope that I have that desire in all I am doing. And I know that if I do this, love will lead me by the right road though I may know nothing about it. Therefore will I trust love always, though I may seem to be lost and in the shadow of death. I will fear, but with love I will also know that I never need face my perils alone.

I will trust love always.

APRIL 24

"To ease another's heartache is to forget one's own."
— Abraham Lincoln

Lots of people we know are also grieving. Our family members, our friends, our neighbors, our coworkers—many of them have also lost someone special in recent months or years.

One of our most important mourning needs is to receive and accept support from others. But reaching out in grief is a two-way street. We are grateful when people reach out to us. We can also activate healing by reaching out to others in grief.

Extending kindness to others is a means of extending kindness to ourselves. It helps them, and it helps us. That's because we are actually one with others. We are all connected, like undifferentiated drops in a single ocean. Practicing empathy heals humanity.

I can help ease another's heartache
and in doing so, ease my own.

APRIL 25

"You can only be young once. But you can always be immature."
— Dave Barry

Have you ever noticed that children instinctively know how to grieve and mourn?

When something they care about is taken away from them, what do they do? They cry and carry on! They throw a tantrum! They sob and wail and kick and scream! That's the most pure, instinctive human response to loss. It's embracing thoughts and feelings in the moment then expressing the heck out of them. It's only as we grow older and "mature" that social norms kick in, forcing us to "keep it together" and "get a grip."

The next time we feel like crying and carrying on, let's. A little natural (and wise) immaturity in grief is a good thing.

I can throw tantrums when I feel like it. Maybe what's widely considered immaturity in grief is actually maturity.

APRIL 26

"Consciousness is only possible through change;
change is only possible through movement."
— Aldous Huxley

When we actively express our inner thoughts and feelings in grief, we put our grief in motion. Mourning creates movement, and movement creates change.

In my grief counseling practice, I call this "perturbation." Basically, we "perturb" our grief by talking about it, writing about it, making art about it, or expressing it any way. We give it a nudge. We "bother" it, if you will.

Perturbation makes our grief interact with life, and it is this interaction that, over time, changes it. Perturbation might initially bother our grief, but eventually it softens it.

Making my grief active—giving it movement—
allows it to change and soften.

APRIL 27

*"Feelings come and go like clouds in a windy sky.
Conscious breathing is my anchor."*

— Thich Nhat Hanh

I'm a big proponent of feeling feelings. That's because over the years, the thousands of mourners I've counseled and learned from have taught me that when they embrace their feelings instead of avoiding or denying them, the feelings begin to soften. It's a simple yet magical alchemy.

But sometimes our feelings of grief can be so overwhelming that in that moment, we need to calm them. If we don't, they'll literally knock us down. When this happens, we can turn to deep breathing. Breathing slowly and deeply is one way to "turn off" our stress reaction to our strong feelings and "turn on" relaxation.

Sit or stand and place your hands on your stomach. Inhale slowly and deeply through your nose, letting your stomach expand as much as possible. When you have breathed in as much as possible, hold your breath for a few seconds before exhaling. With your hands still on your stomach, exhale slowly through your mouth, pursing your lips like you are going to whistle. By pursing your lips, you can control how fast you exhale and keep your airways open as long as possible. When your lungs feel empty, start the cycle again by inhaling and exhaling. Repeat this at least three or four times. Notice how much calmer you feel already.

When my feelings overwhelm me, deep breathing can help calm me.

APRIL 28

"Instead of seeing depression as a dysfunction, it is a functioning phenomenon. It stops you cold, sets you down, makes you damn miserable."

— James Hillman

As someone who has traveled around the world teaching about grief and written lots of books on the subject, I'm often asked about depression. People want to know if depression is normal in grief. They want to know if they're clinically depressed or simply grieving.

Here is what I know: Sadness is a natural, authentic emotion after a loss. In other words, it's normal to be depressed after someone loved dies. The depression of grief plays an essential role. It forces us to turn inward, withdraw, and regroup. We need this time of depression to acknowledge the reality of what has happened and to embrace our pain.

One difference between clinical depression and the depression of "good grief" is that clinically depressed people tend to feel pervasive, ongoing hopelessness and a low sense of self-worth. Another is that grief softens over time, while clinical depression does not. If you think you may be clinically depressed, please see a therapist or physician. Not only does clinical depression put you at risk for a number of additional health problems, it will also likely prevent you from moving forward in your journey through grief.

If I think I might be clinically depressed, I promise to call today to make an appointment with a licensed therapist or physician.

APRIL 29

Eeyore: "We can't all, and some of us don't. That's all there is to it."
Pooh: "Can't all what?"
Eeyore: "Gaiety. Song-and-dance. Here we go
round the mulberry bush."

— A.A. Milne

Eeyore gets that we can't all be happy all of the time. Right now most of us just aren't doing gaiety and song-and-dance. We're experiencing "anhedonia," which is a fancy term for finding no pleasure in things we used to enjoy. Unlike Eeyore, though, we try to hold onto hope for gaiety and song-and-dance in our futures.

Have you ever known someone who always seems unhappy, like Eeyore? Unless there's a serious underlying mental illness, such people use their perpetual grumpiness as a protective mechanism to keep themselves safe. Whether they realize it or not, they choose to be off-putting and negative to avoid the risk of rejection and loss.

Boy, have we ever lost. And—rightfully so—we're feeling grumpy right now. But we also have experienced priceless love and connection, and so we will do our grief work and trust that one day we will be fortunate enough to go round the mulberry bush again.

I can and I will. One day at a time.

APRIL 30

"Whatever you are physically—male or female, strong or weak, ill or healthy—all those things matter less than what your heart contains. If you have the soul of a warrior, you are a warrior. All those other things, they are the glass that contains the lamp, but you are the light inside."

— Cassandra Clare

I often say that grief is, most of all, a spiritual journey. It is our soul's wrestling with the temporary and transitory nature of human life here on earth.

Our souls are the immortal lights inside us. The remainder of the facts of our existence are simply the container for our souls. Our bodies and our careers and our belongings are simply the glass that contains the lamp that is our soul.

The thing is, our love for the person who died lives in our soul. The death seems to threaten to extinguish the light of our souls; our grief is deeply and profoundly painful. But what happens when we consider that our souls may be immortal, including the soul of the person who died, and that love does not end? How do things change when we weigh the possibility that our human existence here on earth is only the temporary container for our souls?

What happens is we become boundless, timeless beings for whom loss is but the blink of an eye.

My soul is the light inside me, and my soul knows the truth. I will listen to it.

MAY 1

"The earth laughs in flowers."
— Ralph Waldo Emerson

When we are grieving, a simple flower can touch us to the quick. One whiff of its fragrance can transport us. We may be swept back to memories of gardens, hospitals, celebrations, or funerals.

When spring flowers emerge, let us remember that though their tender beauty is fleeting, the tenderness they so easily find in our hearts is eternal. It is our love. And even when the blossoms prick us with pain, we will know that it is the pain borne of love. We will know to have gratitude for their love-liness.

When flowers touch my emotions—whether sad, happy, or bittersweet—I will take a moment to feel those feelings and have gratitude for the love beneath them.

MAY 2

*"There are colors in the sky! There are beautiful colors and
more colors! You can double jump up here, double jump!"*
— 11-year-old John, three days before he died of lymphoma

Deathbed visions are such a common experience that at least to
me, it seems more nonsensical *not* to believe
them than to believe them.

Oh sure, I am a product of a medical-model Ph.D. program in
psychology, so I understand the argument that deathbed visions
are simply the biochemical side effect of the brain's shutting-
down process. But as with all things in life, we can choose to
believe in mystery and synchronicity and eternal meaning—
or we can stick to rigid, confining "facts."

I often teach at hospices and hospice conventions, so in
addition to having witnessed the deathbed visions of my own
father and mother, I learn from hospice nurses about their
extremely frequent "paranormal" experiences companioning the
dying. Those nurses emphatically believe. What do you believe?

---

*I can choose to believe that there is, or may be,
something beautiful beyond death.*

MAY 3

"The worst lies are the lies we tell ourselves. We live in denial of what we do, even what we think. We do this because we're afraid."
— Richard Bach

Denial is one of the most misunderstood aspects of the grief journey. Temporarily, denial, like shock and numbness, is a great gift. It helps us survive the early days and weeks after the death of someone loved.

As we begin to confront the reality of the death and embrace the pain in doses, though, our denial should begin to break down. And when that happens, we often feel even worse for some period of time. That's hard to take, but avoiding or "stuffing" our true thoughts and feelings is even more terrible because it inevitably leads to stagnation, depression, anxiety, addictive behaviors, and other life-smothering symptoms. If we're afraid to feel, we can end up feeling worse.

So let's all do the denial dance. Deny, confront, deny, confront. I sometimes call it evade-encounter. This healthy back-and-forth doses us with reality then gives us a much-needed break.

I can deny, set aside, and postpone now and then as long as I'm encountering in between. I'll put my dancing shoes on.

MAY 4

"The world's favorite season is the Spring.
All things seem possible in May."
— Edwin Way Teale

Hope and renewal burst into bloom in May. Where I live, in
Colorado, May means sunshine and green grass, birds
singing and flowers blooming. It's just a little
easier to be hopeful in May.

Sometimes, though, our grief and May seem incongruent.
Inside, we're of necessity dark and dreary, while outside the
world is a riot of color and joy. Especially early in our grief,
there may be cause for skipping May by holing up indoors,
closing the blinds, and sitting in the darkness of our despair.

Mostly, though, May invites us to understand that things can
and will get better. Everything is possible. Hope springs eternal.
It comes frocked in flowers and sunshine.

All things are possible, including healing and future joy.

MAY 5

"Your shoes will make you happy today."
— A fortune cookie

I don't know about you, but whenever I crack open a fortune cookie, I can't help but feel a frisson of anticipation. What will it say? Will it reveal something amazing about my future? I'm not a particularly superstitious person, but I do have a thing for fortune cookies.

One day I unfurled the fortune above, and I chuckled. I looked askance at my brown loafers. They didn't exactly fill me with joy and wonder.

But then I realized: In this fortune, my shoes are just a metaphor for all the little things in my life that I take for granted every day. And if I stop and consider them with the gratitude they deserve, I can essentially manufacture happiness.

I try to remember this fortune on days when my grief is pulling me under. If I try, I can find gratitude for my favorite reading chair, my daughter's text, my wife's smile, and yes, even my shoes.

I will try to notice and muster gratitude for at least three everyday things today.

MAY 6

"I can't go on. I'll go on."
— Samuel Becket

Some days we feel we can't possibly go on. Living in grief is just too hard. We are mired in pain and despair. Yet somehow we go on. The earth keeps spinning. We make it through the day, and the night. And the sun rises again. We have survived. Some days that is enough.

Yet even in our darkest days of just surviving, we may see glimmers of hope. We may feel tugs of connection with others. We may even experience brief twinges of joy. It is for these glimmers, tugs, and twinges that we will go on. And if we actively mourn, we can trust there will be more and more such moments in our future, until slowly they make up the bulk of our days and our grief becomes the thing that glimmers, tugs, and twinges in the background.

*When I feel that I can't go on, I will express my grief
and actively notice glimmers of hope,
tugs of connection, and twinges of joy.*

MAY 7

"You are the average of the five people you spend the most time with."
— Jim Rohn

I'm not convinced the math can be calculated so precisely, but it's true that the quality of our lives is greatly influenced by the people we spend the most time with.

When we're grieving, the quality of our healing is greatly influenced by those people. If we're surrounded by compassionate companions who allow us to grieve as we need to grieve and openly express our true thoughts and feelings without judging or trying to take them away from us, we are being helped toward healing. If, on the other hand, we are surrounded by people who ignore our grief and mourning, respond with "carry on and keep your chin up" types of messages, or, worse yet, shame us for our thoughts and feelings, we are being knocked off the path toward healing.

If you find yourself among the latter crowd, try spending less time with them and finding more of the former folks to hang around with. This one change can make all the difference.

I deserve to be helped through my time of grief by compassionate, nonjudgmental people. I will make an effort to spend more time with people who fit this description.

MAY 8

"I cannot forget my mother. She is my bridge. When I needed to get across, she steadied herself long enough for me to run across safely."
— Renita Weems

When we were children and something went wrong, most of us ran to our mothers. Our mothers kissed away the hurt and made everything better. They weren't perfect (no one is), but often more than anyone else in the whole world, they actively loved us.

Now we're experiencing a kind of hurt that our moms can't heal. For some of us, our mothers have died and have become a source of our grief. For others, our mothers are no longer integral parts of our daily lives, are far away, and/or are no longer able to be our champions.

My own mother died five years ago, after a several-year-long struggle with dementia. Sometimes when I miss her, I still like to remember the days when I was a child and she made everything better. In those precious memories I am immersed in the knowing that I was loved beyond measure.
What more could I ask for?

I remember my mother, father, or other grown-ups who loved me when I was a child. I can take refuge in these memories.

MAY 9

"I think it pisses God off if you walk by the color purple in a field somewhere and don't notice it. People think pleasing God is all God cares about. But any fool living in the world can see it always trying to please us back."

— Alice Walker

For many of us, questioning and getting mad at God over the death of the person we love is a natural and necessary part of our grief journeys. If God loves us, why did this happen? Why do bad things happen to good people?

Just maybe, though, as Alice Walker suggests, God is all over the place trying to make us feel better. Maybe He's showing us that pretty sunrise and that stunning tree and that baby's smile and that purple flower just to console us. And also maybe as a glimpse—a foreshadowing, if you will— of the glory to come.

It's OK to question God. He can take it. But at the same time, maybe we can also work on noticing and having gratitude for the miracles He's scattered so generously all around us.

I will work on noticing the purple flowers and the blessings around me.

MAY 10

*"Don't wish away your problems. They need action,
not wishful thinking."*

— Bangambiki Habyarimana

When I was a child and I wished for things, my mother would sometimes quote from a nursery rhyme. "If wishes were horses," she would say, "beggars would ride." Wishes don't change reality, she was telling me. But now that I'm much older and wiser, I understand that she wasn't quite right.

Wishes that are used to fuel action *do* effect change. They're the intention behind the doing. In grief, our wishes that we could feel better, that we could go one day without crying, that we could experience joy again, can all be moved into reality through active mourning.

What's more, wishes can be understood as the hopes and expectations we bring to our lives. Many great philosophers believe that our thoughts create reality. So, if we wish for something and believe it can be so, maybe it's true that we are aligning with the mysterious energies of the universe that guide the unrolling future.

*I wish my grief would soften. I hope and believe that
through active mourning, it will.*

MAY 11

"We need time to dream, time to remember, time to reach for the infinite. Time to be."
— Gladys Taber

It's hard to understand until we ourselves experience our first Great Grief, but grief takes time. It takes a LOT of time. It consumes whole chunks of our days and weeks. And as time spools forward, it takes months and years for us to express, accommodate, and learn to live with.

But let's remind ourselves that grieving and mourning are two of the most meaningful ways we can spend our time. We get so caught up in the constant connectedness of modern life—checking social media, answering texts, binge watching TV shows—that we are at risk for believing that *those* activities are the important ones. They are not.

Like its counterpart, love, grief requires time to dream, remember, reach for the infinite, and simply be. So let's not feel bad or guilty when our grief consumes our days.

I need time to grieve and mourn. I will prioritize this time.

MAY 12

"Earth has no sorrow that Earth cannot heal."
— John Muir

Many of us find nature's timeless beauty healing—if we only allow ourselves to unplug and detach. The sound of a bird singing or the awesome presence of an old tree can help put things in perspective. Mother Earth knows more about kicking back than all the stress management experts on the planet—and she charges far less.

I recall a recent afternoon when I was feeling overwhelmed and went for a walk. I saw beautiful flowers. I saw leaves falling from the trees. I watched my Husky dogs leap with joy. I took long, deep breaths. I felt a sense of gratitude. After just a few minutes outdoors, I felt renewed, changed.

If you're lucky enough to be able to travel or hike far away from civilization now and then, you may well find that your grief takes on a more manageable shape in such miraculous places. But even stepping outdoors and sitting on a park bench in the middle of a crowded city gives you access to nature's capacity to heal.

I will step out today and breathe deeply. I will observe all the sights and focus on the sounds. I will spend some time marveling at the miracle that is unfolding right outside my door.

MAY 13

"The opposite of love is not hate, it's indifference. The opposite of art is not ugliness, it's indifference. The opposite of faith is not heresy, it's indifference. And the opposite of life is not death, it's indifference."

— Elie Wiesel

I often say that people who refuse to acknowledge and embrace their grief are not really and truly avoiding the hurt. Instead, they are choosing to die while they are alive. In denying their essential thoughts and feelings, they are throwing a blanket over their divine sparks. They are building a wall between themselves and everything that is most meaningful in life.

The opposite of grief is not joy, it's indifference. It's the false, half-life of trying to protect ourselves from pain. The only way to block out pain is to block out all strong emotions and emotional experiences, good and bad.

We grieve and mourn so that we can love and live again.

The opposite of grief is not joy, it's indifference. Muting my grief mutes my soul.

MAY 14

*"Three things are fundamental to an understanding of mourning.
First, each loss launches us on an inescapable course through grief.
Second, each loss revives all past losses. Third, each loss, if fully
mourned, can be a vehicle for growth and regeneration."*
— Vamik D. Volkan, M.D.

Such a simple, elegant summary. Such a complex,
messy thing to actually do.

Dr. Volkan is right, of course. Grief is unavoidable. Each new
grief reawakens all old griefs, because they are linked together
in the chain of our life stories. And active mourning leads
to a new and enriched wholeness.

In the chaos of our grief, we can remember this rule of three.
It is the tripod that will hold us steady no matter
how we are shaken.

*When my grief is feeling chaotic and out of control, I will call to
mind these three fundamentals. They embody my trust in the
mourning process and my hope for the future.*

MAY 15

"Life is a great big canvas. Throw all the paint on it that you can."
— Danny Kaye

Grief is a great big canvas too. It's got room for everything we are thinking and feeling.

So let's throw all the paint on it that we can. Let's take what's inside of us and express it outside of us, never worrying about what it's going to look like. Let's get messy and splotchy and wild.

When we're through the worst of our grief, we'll look at our canvas and realize, "Whaddya know. We put it all out there, and we created a masterpiece."

I'm gonna throw all the paint on the canvas of my grief that I can.

MAY 16

"Do I not destroy my enemies by making them my friends?"
— Abraham Lincoln

Our culture tends to think of grief as the enemy. It's bad.
We want to ignore it or at least get rid of it as soon as we can.

But as we're learning, this is a misconception. What we really
need to do is befriend our grief. We need to hold it close,
empathize with it, and try to understand it. We need
to regard it with, well, love.

We don't really destroy our grief by making it our friend,
though. Instead, we come to accept it as part of us. If love is the
yang of our lives, grief is the yin. They are not opposing forces;
they are complementary. In befriending our grief, the only thing
we destroy is the misconception that it is our enemy.

*I will befriend my grief and in doing so,
learn that it is not my enemy.*

MAY 17

*"Such a tapestry of memories we weave throughout our lives. Even
when there is unevenness, variations, or faults within the
weaving process, the result is still beautiful."*

— Linda K. Peterson

Like our presents and our futures, our pasts are filled with all
kinds of people and experiences. Life is largely unpredictable
and uncontrollable. And so, despite our often rosy plans and the
usually good intentions of those around us, we end up with a
mishmash of formative experiences and memories.

Our memories of the person who died are part of this
mishmash. They may range from joyful to tender to infuriating
to blasé to cold to contented to downright ugly. But such is the
patchwork of life! When you examine any one square up close,
you may find it discouraging or hurtful. But when you step back
to see the entire crazy quilt—it's beautiful beyond measure.

*If I find myself struggling with unpleasant memories or regrets,
I'll try to take a step back to see the bigger picture.
Life is imperfectly, breathtakingly beautiful.*

MAY 18

"Work when there is work to do. Rest when you are tired. One thing done in peace will most likely be better than ten things done in panic. I am not a hero if I deny rest; I am only tired."

— Susan McHenry

We have much grief work to do. But it's fatiguing! We get so, so tired.

We need to rest as much as we need to do our grief work. Rest is not only sleeping or simply lying down; it also includes allowing ourselves times of entertainment and distraction. Trying to do all our grief work in a panic is counterproductive.

We mourn. We rest. We rest. We mourn a bit again. Then we rest. There are no rewards for speed. This is the natural and necessary rhythm of our lives right now.

When I am tired, I will rest. There are no rewards for speed.

MAY 19

"Come on, don't you ever stop and smell the coffee?"
— Justina Chen

For many of us, coffee is a daily ritual. We've grown to need the caffeine, but we also revel in the smell of the beans, the *grrr* of the grinding, and the drip (or press) of the brew.

Our daily rituals can hold us up and sustain us during our time of grief. We may be disorganized, discombobulated, and disheveled, but we still have the muscle memory to make a pot of coffee or step into line at our favorite coffeehouse. Reading the morning news (whether online or in print), watching our TV shows, walking to get the mail, checking our email…we can rely on and have gratitude for any routines that help us get through the day.

It's also OK to drop any daily rituals we don't feel up to for the time being. When our grief makes our energy levels low, we may simply need to lie down and be still. But thank goodness for those rituals that (forgive the pun) ground us.

My daily rituals are handholds to healing.

MAY 20

*"The soul always knows what to do to heal itself.
The challenge is to silence the mind."*

— Caroline Myss

Have you heard of the phrase "monkey mind"? It's a Buddhist term for our mind's tendency to think, think, think, constantly chattering random thoughts at us. Many of our thoughts are benign observations—*Look at that cute kitten on Facebook!*—but lots of others are fears and worries—*I'm going to miss my plane! The doctor will find something bad! I'm never going to feel happy again!*

Learning to stop paying attention to our monkey minds helps us move toward healing our grief. Mindfulness practices such as yoga and meditation teach us to ignore our monkeys. So do activities like spending time in nature and getting physical (sports, walking the dog, gardening, etc.).

Our monkeys aren't our friends in grief, but if we can tame them a bit, we'll see that in the silence and peace we open up, our souls know what to do.

When my monkeys are bothering me, I'll work on ways to quiet them so I can hear my soul speak.

MAY 21

"Awake, my dear.
Be kind to your sleeping heart.
Take it out into the vast fields of Light
and let it breathe."

— Hafiz

Loss shakes our hearts awake. "Wake up!" it says. "You've been asleep…taking the special relationships in your life for granted and spending time on things that don't matter. Wake up!"

Now our awakened hearts are hurting. We must be kind to them. Mindful grieving, mourning, and living require tenderness and self-compassion.

And so we take our awakened hearts out into the vast fields of Light. We expose them to the truth—to love, to kindness, to spirituality, to contemplation. We break them free from the dark cave where we have been hiding them, and we let them breathe.

My heart was sleeping, but now that it is awake,
I will be kind to it.

MAY 22

*"There are only two days in the year that nothing can be done. One is
called yesterday and the other is called tomorrow, so today is the
right day to love, believe, do, and mostly live."*

— Dalai Lama XIV

We grievers spend a lot of time thinking back on our yesterdays.
It's normal and necessary for us to remember. We also spend
a lot of time thinking—and worrying—about our tomorrows.
How will I go on living? What will happen next month/year?
These thoughts are also normal and necessary.

Yet it's also true that today is when our life is happening. As
Eckhart Tolle says, nothing happened yesterday—it happened
in the Now. Nothing will happen tomorrow—
it will happen in the Now.

We must find a balance in our remembering and forecasting,
also allowing plenty of time for living today.

I will focus today on living, on purpose, in the Now.

MAY 23

"Questions wake people up. They prompt new ideas. They show
people new places, new ways of doing things."
— Michael Marquardt

Have you noticed that grief brings with it a
boatload of questions?

We have so many "why?" and "how?" questions.
Why did this have to happen? Why now, in this way?
Then: How will I go on?

Other people have questions for us, too. How are you doing?
What happened? What are you going to do next?
Their need to know can be exhausting.

For the time being, there may be more questions than answers.
Questioning is part of the grief journey. All of the questions
make us consider what we think, feel, believe. The questions—
even when there are no answers—wake us up.

I've got questions. So do others. It's normal and natural to ask,
even when answers aren't forthcoming or easy.

MAY 24

"There are only two ways to live your life. One is as though nothing is a miracle. The other is as though everything is a miracle."

— Albert Einstein

Do you ever stare at those optical illusion drawings—the ones that look like one thing at first glance, but if you keep looking, your brain adjusts and you can see a different image?

That's kind of what Albert Einstein is talking about here. We might see much of our lives as mundane or, worse yet, disappointing or tragic. But we can choose to look at the very same things and see, instead, wonder and joy.

As with the optical illusion trick, seeing everything as a miracle might take some time and practice. If we're depressed or accustomed to pessimism, it's harder…
but still very much possible.

Love is a miracle. Life is a miracle. Even death and grief are miracles. Everything is a miracle.

If love is a miracle, then grief is a miracle too.

MAY 25

"Memory is a way of holding onto the things you love,
the things you are, the things you never want to lose."
— The Wonder Years

Especially in our early grief, our memories can be painful.
Joyous and minor memories alike only seem to
remind us of what we have lost.

But over time we learn that our memories are our most precious
keepsakes. In remembering and in sharing those memories with
others, we honor the person who died. We acknowledge the un-
erasableness of our love. And we imbue the current
moment with the meaning of the past.

If I am ever told to "move on" or forget my past, I will remember
this: It is in listening to the music of the past that I can sing
in the present and dance into the future.

MAY 26

*"One of the most calming and powerful actions you can do to
intervene in a stormy world is to stand up and show your soul."*
— Clarissa Pinkola Estes

Grief is first and foremost a spiritual journey. Matters of life
and death are spiritual challenges. We struggle physically,
cognitively, emotionally, and socially, too—
but most of all, spiritually.

That's why first getting in touch with and then revealing our
souls are such powerful actions in grief. Our love lives there.
Which means our grief lives there also. Connecting with the
authentic Truths inside us and taking actions congruent
with those Truths is what mourning is all about.

When our grief and our lives are stormy, let's stand up and show
our souls. Such transparency makes us vulnerable, it's true…
but there's also a calm and power in genuineness.

When my grief is stormy, I will stand up and show my soul.

MAY 27

*"Until one loves an animal, a part of one's soul
remains unawakened."*

— Anatole France

Those of us who are pet lovers know how much our companion animals help us when we are grieving. They are such a comforting part of our lives. Their physical presence and unconditional love help us survive and heal.

I myself have been a dog owner for decades. Whenever I am feeling low, I know I can leash up my canine companions and we can go for a walk or head to the dog park, where I'm sure to encounter not only fresh air, sunshine, and joyful doggy antics but also the company of other humans.

My editor is a cat lover, and she swears that the purr of her lap cats lowers her stress and is the very soundtrack of peace.

If you don't have a pet, maybe now's the time to consider adopting one. You'll never find a more loyal and sensitive grief companion.

*I can cry and be myself with my pets.
Every moment I'm with them is time well spent.*

MAY 28

"I wanted a perfect ending. Now I've learned, the hard way, that some poems don't rhyme, and some stories don't have a clear beginning, middle, and end. Life is about not knowing, having to change, taking the moment, and making the best of it, without knowing what's going to happen next. Delicious Ambiguity."

— Gilda Radner

It's natural to want a perfect ending, but instead life throws curveballs. Some of the curveballs we like, some we don't. Life is about the unexpected. It's about grieving then accommodating change.

You might recall that Saturday Night Live comedian Gilda Radner died of ovarian cancer at the age of 42. In her dying, she came to appreciate the deliciousness of ambiguity. Of not knowing what might happen tomorrow. Of living in a constant state of flux and uncertainty.

We don't like living in flux and uncertainty; we're built to prefer the safety of certainty, probably because we as a species evolved from a time long ago when daily uncertainty often meant life or death. The most primal parts of our brains are built for fight or flight. But now that our day-to-day lives are generally safe, we can use our higher-order thinking to calm our lizard brains and to cultivate an appreciation for flux and change.
For Delicious Ambiguity.

I am learning to grieve change while also cultivating an appreciation for Delicious Ambiguity.

MAY 29

"I do believe in an everyday sort of magic—the inexplicable connectedness we sometimes experience with places, people, works of art and the like; the eerie appropriateness of moments of synchronicity; the whispered voice, the hidden presence, when we think we're alone."

— Charles de Lint

If we allow it to, our grief sharpens our awareness. It turns our attention to lots of little signs and synchronicities we may have overlooked before.

I think this happens in part because in grief, we're newly on high alert. We're searching for the people who died. Our minds are trying to figure out where they've gone.

And who knows, maybe our enhanced perception is the very thing that allows us to sense their hidden presence. It's like our grief comes equipped with a highly sensitive detection system just when we need it most.

I can embrace the magic of synchronicities and hidden presences, especially if I find comfort in them.

MAY 30

"Friends are the bacon bits in the salad bowl of life."
— Author Unknown

If you're a vegetarian, maybe substitute "heirloom tomatoes"
or "candied pecans" for "bacon bits."

The point is, life is a crazy, mixed-up mishmash of ingredients
all tossed together. And the people we love are the
extremely special, very best parts.

Our compassionate, good-listener friends and family members
are the bacon bits in the salad bowl of grief. They are the bits
of kindness and happiness in our days of despair.

The catch is, we have to let our friends into our salad bowls. If
we don't, we're bacon bitless. And what a shame would that be?

I need some bacon bits today. I'll make sure I get some.

MAY 31

"The pain I feel now is the happiness I had before. That's the deal."
— C.S. Lewis

Our worst days of grief can make it seem like a terrible deal. We love so much and experience such happiness and fulfillment in our love…only to be dashed on the very shores of our love. Sometimes love—the purpose and essence of life— feels like a cruel bargain.

All we can do is keep loving. Because the ultimate paradox is this: Love leads to grief, but only love can quell grief. In continuing to love the person who died, we soften our grief. In reaching out to others for connection and love, we soften our grief.

We rebuild our shores with love. Love is the question, and love is the answer.

I will love and allow myself to be loved. Yes, love is the source of my pain, but it is also the transcendence from my pain.

JUNE 1

*"Grief is like manure. If you spread it out, it fertilizes.
If you leave it in a big pile, it smells like crap."*
— Tom Golden

By all means, then, let's spread out our grief.
We do that in two ways.

One essential way is by actively mourning. If our grief is a big lump inside of us, we spread it out by expressing it daily outside of ourselves. We seek out ways to declare our thoughts and feelings and take advantage of such opportunities when they arise by happenstance. We let it out, piece by piece.

The other way we spread out our grief is by dosing ourselves with it. We can't take on all of our grief at once. It's too big, too painful, and too powerful. So we spread it out, encountering it a bit at a time and allowing ourselves to retreat from it the rest of the time. We're not denying; we're surviving.
This, too, is normal and necessary.

I will spread out my grief through mourning and dosing. In these ways my grief will ultimately make my life richer and more lush.

JUNE 2

"It is now, in this world, that we must live."
— Andre Gide

Some days we hate this truth. After all, this is the world in which people die. This is the world lacking the person we love. We hate this world sometimes.

But Andre Gide won the Nobel Prize for literature in 1947, so I suppose he knows what he's talking about. Notice his use of the word "must." He's saying that we don't have a choice. We *have* to live now, in this world.

Yet I noticed there's another way of reading his admonition. He could also be encouraging us to truly live, not just survive. We must live! Life is a miraculous opportunity! Yes, I think I will choose to agree with him on that score today.

I am in this world this day, and so I will live it.

JUNE 3

"Let everything happen to you: beauty and terror.
Just keep going. No feeling is final."
— Rainer Maria Rilke

No feeling is final, but what we feel now in this time of our grief seems like it is. Our sadness, despair, and other dark emotions threaten to go on and on and on. We fear the unrelenting pain will never end.

Yet the pain will soften. If we mourn honestly and fully, over time our hurt will ease. It will never disappear completely but instead become a thread in the fabric of our loving, meaningful, continued living.

Oh, and—Rilke is not completely right. Our love for the person who died is a feeling that is final. This is another truth we can hold onto.

In the midst of my despair I will hold onto the faith that the pain I feel now will eventually ease. I will keep going, knowing that the hurt will soften and the love will remain.

JUNE 4

"I like nonsense. It wakes up the brain cells. Fantasy is a necessary ingredient in living; it's a way of looking at life through the wrong end of a telescope—and that enables you to laugh at life's realities."

— Dr. Seuss

Isn't life absurd? Things happen all the time—big things!—that simply make no sense. The story of our special person's death might be one of those things.

Our brains are wired to look for patterns and make sense of things; that's why we're often uncomfortable about things that can't be logically explained.

We can do what Dr. Seuss did, though. We can pick up our telescopes and look through the wrong end. We can learn to laugh at much of life's nonsense—or at least not let it drag us under. Wouldn't it do all of us good to work to be a little more like Dr. Seuss?

Nonsense can be fun and good for me. I'll try to remember that.

JUNE 5

*"The great thing about new friends is that they bring
new energy to your soul."*
— Shanna Rodriguez

Meeting new people when we're grieving is one way
to give our grief momentum.

It's the newness itself that provides the opportunity. The
freshness of the encounter stimulates our minds, hearts, and
souls. This new energy forces us to think, communicate,
and often, tell our stories.

Plus, we never know what new people will bring into our lives.
Sometimes it's the very thing we need to get unstuck
or ease today's pain.

Support groups, clubs, spiritual groups, community
volunteering, travel, even saying hello to those we bump into
in our communities—all these and more are ways to meet
new people. When we're ready, we will open ourselves to
the blessings they can bring to our lives.

Meeting new people can give my grief momentum.

JUNE 6

*"The reality is that you will grieve forever. You will not 'get over' the
loss of a loved one; you will learn to live with it. You will heal and you
will rebuild yourself around the loss you have suffered. You will be
whole again, but you will never be the same. Nor should
you be the same nor would you want to."*

— Elisabeth Kübler-Ross

Whenever we enter into a relationship with another human
being, we are changed. The time we spend together and the
love we share changes both of us. He or she becomes an
inextricable part of the mosaic of our lives.

But then this person dies. A piece of the mosaic grows lifeless,
yet notice that it does not disappear. Though it is different
now, it is still cemented into place. It will always
remain part of who we are.

Thank goodness. If our love died at the moment our special
people died, what an empty existence this would be.

*I will try to find gratitude for my grief because it means I still love.
I will continue building the mosaic of my life even as I recognize
that loss and grief are inextricable parts of the mosaic.*

JUNE 7

"All forgiveness is a gift to yourself."
— Marianne Williamson

The person who died might have done things that hurt us. Since the death, other people might have offended us or acted badly. We might even be mad at ourselves.

Forgiveness in grief is a tricky thing. I'm not one of those people who thinks you *must* forgive; some human transgressions are simply unforgiveable in my book. In those cases, it's OK not to forgive. Forgiveness is not a requirement for healing.

But (and this is one of those big buts), for many mourners, forgiveness is an important milestone in their journeys through grief. When they are finally able to forgive, they feel relieved of a heavy burden. As Marianne Williamson suggests, they realize that in forgiving, they have given themselves a gift.

If we harbor anger and resentment, let's try on forgiveness and see how it feels. If and when it feels right, we will likely find that it gives our grief a welcome burst of forward momentum.

I can choose to give myself the gift of forgiveness any time I feel the urge.

JUNE 8

"God offers us a yearly necklace of twelve pearls; most men choose the fairest, label it June, and cast the rest away."

— Thomas Wentworth Higginson

June is often the fairest month here in Colorado. The days are warm, the skies are blue, the flowers are lush, and the nights are still a bit crisp. The days of June are also long, giving us 16 or so hours of golden sunlight each day.

Depending on where we are in our grief journeys, we may not be in a position to admire June. Or we may be emerging just enough from our darkness to appreciate her beauty.

I have spent many Junes in wonder but at least several in despair. Regardless, I know that June is outside waiting for me, always ready to extend me her hope and healing. And I trust that even when I am in no position to commune with her, she will return next year, unoffended by my temporary absence and without fail unfurling anew her splendor.

I may miss certain moments of healing wonder during my time of intense grief. But I needn't fret, for I can trust that I will have the opportunity to experience more such moments in my future.

JUNE 9

*"Remember that you come into this world in the middle of the movie,
and you leave in the middle; and so do the people you love.
Love never dies, and spirit knows no loss."*

— Louise Hay

We tend to think in terms of our life spans here on earth. One hundred years—we all understand this as a long, full life, and we generally consider anything less than 80 or so years a life cut short. So when someone we love who is younger dies, we grieve doubly. We grieve the loss, and we grieve the years together we were robbed of.

Maybe we can shift our thinking. Maybe we can think of our lives as infinite. Maybe we existed before our blink of time on earth, and maybe we continue to exist after. What hope this understanding offers!

I am on this earth, but I am not of this earth. Deep down, my spirit knows this. When I am struggling with loss, I will consider the eternalness of love and the reunion I hope to one day experience with those who have gone before me.

JUNE 10

"If one dream should fall and break into a thousand pieces, never be afraid to pick one of those pieces up and begin again."
—Flavia Weedn

Our dreams lie shattered. They've broken
into a thousand pieces.

We can't pick up the pieces and put them back together exactly as they were. The seams will show, for one thing. For another, there are so many pieces that we can't possibly reassemble our dreams just as they were.

We can, though, pick up one special piece. We can use it as the starting point for a new or revised dream.

Starting with one piece, I can begin again.

JUNE 11

"Grief can be the garden of compassion. If you keep your heart open through everything, your pain can become your greatest ally in your life's search for love and wisdom."

— Rumi

Our grief is not only our friend; it is our ally. It has our best interests at heart. It looks out for us and wants only what's best for us.

If we're wise, what do we do with allies? We listen to them. We seek their counsel. We hold their opinions in the highest regard.

Our grief knows what to do and when to do it. We can trust it to guide us toward our most meaningful and joyous future.

My grief is my greatest ally.

JUNE 12

"Every day my love for you grows higher, deeper, wider, stronger... It grows and grows until it touches the tip of where you are and comes back to me in the loving memory of you, and my heart melts with that love and grows even more."

— Maureen Hunter

We never stop loving our special people who have died. In fact, as we grow older and wiser, we often gain the maturity and perspective to understand just how precious that relationship was…and our love grows. Our cup runneth over.

Sometimes the question becomes: what to do with our abundant love? The object of our love is not here for us to lavish attention on. Maybe we could share it with someone else. Perhaps a friend, family member, or neighbor could really use some of our loving kindness right now. Or how about volunteering for a cause or nonprofit that was meaningful to the person who died?

The amazing thing is that love shared does not diminish— it multiplies.

I appreciate the love we shared so much. The more I remember with gratitude, the bigger my love gets. When it overflows, I'll find ways to share it that would make you smile.

JUNE 13

*"It is a curious thing, the death of a loved one. We all know that our
time in this world is limited, and that eventually all of us will end
up underneath some sheet, never to wake up. And yet it is always a
surprise when it happens to someone we know. It is like walking up
the stairs to your bedroom in the dark, and thinking there is one more
stair than there is. Your foot falls down, through the air, and there is
a sickly moment of dark surprise as you try and readjust
the way you thought of things."*

— Lemony Snicket

It's true. The death of our loved ones caught us off guard. Even
if we'd been expecting the death for a while, the actual
death was still a dark surprise.

Not yet! Not now! Stop! We're never ready.

The shock comes from the finality. Death is a line that, once
crossed, can't be uncrossed. There is no going back. We're
not able to grasp that, not really, until it happens.

It takes time and hard work to readjust after the
sickly moment of surprise.

**Feeling shock and surprise after someone dies is normal.
It will take time and hard work to readjust.**

JUNE 14

"Pain removes the veil; it plants the flag of truth within the fortress of a rebel soul."

— C.S. Lewis

Our pain strips us of pretense and frippery. It forces us to look at the purest, barest truths of our existence. What do we really care about? Whom do we love? What makes our continuing lives worth living?

Our grief is painful. The stripping-away process is also painful. It's hard to examine our lives and realize that we're not dedicating our time, money, and attention to things that really matter to us. It can be excruciating to abandon people and pastimes we had long been attached to…but only out of habit.

The flag of truth is a symbol worth committing our allegiance to, though. Now that our grief has revealed it to us, do we really have a choice but to follow it?

My pain has revealed to me what is true and important. I am making changes in my life based on this revelation.

JUNE 15

*"You will lose someone you can't live without, and your heart will
be badly broken, and the bad news is that you never completely get
over the loss of your beloved. But this is also the good news. They live
forever in your broken heart that doesn't seal back up. And you come
through. It's like having a broken leg that never heals perfectly—
that still hurts when the weather gets cold, but you
learn to dance with the limp."*

— Anne Lamott

Our hearts are so badly broken we know they will never be as
they were. If we do our work of mourning, our brokenness will
heal, but it will heal imperfectly. We are torn apart, and what
is torn into raggedy edges can only ever be patched
and darned. The patches will always show.

But over time, we will grow to understand that our brokenness
is part of our wholeness. Our love lives in the torn places, so we
wouldn't want those spots to disappear. Actually, our love and
grief knit together to form a patch. And while the patches are
imperfect, they tell the most beautiful stories of our lives.

---

*Just like the scars on my body, the scars in my heart tell the
stories of my life. I choose scars over an unscarred, loveless life.*

JUNE 16

*"One of the most beneficial and valuable gifts we can give to ourselves
in this life is allowing ourselves to be surprised. It is okay
if life surprises you. It's a good thing!"*
— C. JoyBell C.

Has your grief surprised you sometimes? Mine has. Seemingly
out of nowhere I'll feel a surge of anger or an excruciating
plunge of despair. Other times I might experience a moment of
giddy laughter. I can be surprised by both the intensity of
my unbidden feelings and their nature.

The rollercoaster of our grief can be disconcerting, but learning
to embrace whatever comes up is one of our
most important tasks.

Life will surprise us in all kinds of ways. That's what it does.
Cultivating an appreciation for surprise makes our lives better.

*If I'm not good at surprises already, I can learn to be.
Resilience is a skill that improves with conscious practice.*

JUNE 17

"The world turns and the world spins, the tide runs in and the tide runs out, and there is nothing in the world more beautiful and more wonderful in all its evolved forms than two souls who look at each other straight on. And there is nothing more woeful and soul-saddening than when they are parted...everything in the world rejoices in the touch, and everything in the world laments in the losing."

— Gary D. Schmidt

There is nothing more beautiful and more wonderful than the love we share with the special people in our loves. When one of them dies, there is nothing more woeful and soul-saddening.

We are woeful. Our souls are saddened.

As the world continues to turn and the tides keep up their back-and-forth, we can reach out to the other people in our lives. Nothing will ever fill the particular absence we feel, but we can meet up with a different soul and look at each other straight on. We can be fully present to one another, and the other person can companion us in our grief.

I lament in the losing. Sharing my grief with a friend or family member today will help me honor the beauty and wonder of the love I still feel and acknowledge the losing.

JUNE 18

"My father used to play with my brother and me in the yard. Mother would come out and say, 'You're tearing up the grass.' 'We're not raising grass,' Dad would reply. 'We're raising boys.'"

— Harmon Killebrew

Several of my childhood friends came to the visitation for my father's funeral. I hadn't seen them for decades. "We loved your dad," they reminded me. "He was the only adult in the neighborhood who let us play in the street. He always said, 'The cars will stop. Go out for a pass.'"

For good and bad, our parents profoundly impact who we become. They pass along their values and their prejudices, their passions and their dislikes. From them we learn how to move, communicate, and love. Usually unknowingly, they also teach us how to grieve and mourn.

I was lucky. Equipped with a good old-fashioned German work ethic, my father was at work much of the time, but when he was home, he was loving and attentive. From him I learned kindness and integrity—both helpful qualities in grief. He is one of the significant people in my life for whom I grieve each and every day. I miss you, Dad.

My parents taught me how to grieve and how to be. I can choose to embrace the helpful parts of their teachings and abandon those that do not serve me well.

JUNE 19

"Laugh. Laugh as much as you can. Laugh until you cry. Cry until you laugh. Keep doing it even if people are passing you on the street saying, 'I can't tell if that person is laughing or crying, but either way they seem crazy. Let's walk faster.' Emote. It's okay. It shows you are thinking and feeling."

— Ellen DeGeneres

Do you ever wonder what would happen if we were all encouraged and trained from a young age to keep showing our emotions and expressing our every thought, just as we did when we were little? To never start "filtering"? Wow, would life be different. There would be some TMI (Too Much Information) going on, that's for sure. But there would also be honesty. Transparency. Truth.

Now what if we were also taught to actively listen to and empathize with others? To bear witness to their pain? To "be with" and accept them no matter what? I believe life on earth would be utterly transformed.

Unfortunately, we don't live in such a world. But one by one, we can claim our right to emote and to have empathy for others' emotions. It's good for us, and it's good for our world.

I can laugh when I feel like laughing, and cry when I feel like crying. No matter the feeling, I can emote.

JUNE 20

"When you look for the good in others,
you discover the best in yourself."

— Martin Walsh

Our grief makes us appropriately inward-focused, especially in the beginning. But when we start venturing out into the world again, looking for the good in everyone we meet is a practice that connects our personal stories of love and loss to the stories of everyone in humanity.

Whenever I meet people, even in quick transactions such as checking out groceries, I try to look them in the eye, smile, and really acknowledge them. I slow down and open myself to their unique individuality. If we have a brief conversation, I try to be genuinely curious as well as forthcoming. I also try to assume the best of them and withhold judgment.

This open, nonjudgmental way of interrelating with strangers (and acquaintances, too!) acknowledges our shared humanity. It activates mutual empathy and releases endorphins. It takes practice, especially for introverts, but it's a ritual that can become a habit, and once ingrained, can transform our experience of life.

I will acknowledge others and look for the
unique and the good in them.

JUNE 21

"Next time a sunrise steals your breath or a meadow of flowers leaves you speechless, remain that way. Say nothing and listen as heaven whispers, 'Do you like it? I did it just for you.'"

— Max Lucado

Even in the midst of our deepest grief, we can be touched by a moment of beauty, joy, or love. When this happens, let's stop to marvel! It takes mindful discipline for many of us to take even a short break from our busy lives, but the more we practice, the more of a habit it will become.

Stop what you're doing. Give your full attention to whatever is creating the feeling of awe, joy, or love in you. If it's another person, speak a kind word of appreciation. If it's a beautiful sight, watch it for a while. If it's a sound, pause and listen. You get the idea.

Did you know that attention is a form of currency? That's why we use the phrase "paying attention." Whatever we spend our precious attention on grows. Attending to moments of beauty, joy, and love will not take away our grief. Nothing can. But it will make our feelings of awe, joy, and love grow. Learning to truly live even as we grieve and mourn is a worthwhile practice.

When I experience moments of awe, joy, or love today, I will stop and pay attention.

JUNE 22

"Never underestimate the healing power of silliness and absurdity."
- Steve Maraboli

A three-year-old and his dad walked down the street to see their neighbor's new litter of kittens. When they returned home, the boy told the mom there were two boy kittens and two girl kittens. "How do you know?" she asked the boy. "Because Dad picked them up and looked underneath," said the boy. "It's printed on the bottom."

I don't know about you, but I like a little silliness with my sadness. And if it's not naturally occurring in my life, I seek it out. I watch a screwball comedy movie, or I click around to find funny clips and memes online.

Hanging out with little kids always provides a good dose of silly. Have you ever noticed how children are silliness experts? We could all learn from them.

Silliness is a close cousin to joy. Welcoming the first leads to experiencing bursts of the latter.

I need the healing power of silliness during my time of grief.

JUNE 23

"Imaginary obstacles are insurmountable. Real ones aren't. But you can't tell the difference when you have no real information. Fear can create even more imaginary obstacles than ignorance can. That's why the smallest step away from speculation and into reality can be an amazing relief."
— Barbara Sher

The fear of grief can be crippling. It's natural to worry—about how we'll go on, about what will happen next, about how others affected by the death will cope. But sometimes the worry looms too large. It takes over, rendering us incapable of feeling or doing anything else.

Usually when fear and worry are dominating, it's because we're suffering from "dirty pain." "Clean pain" is the normal pain that follows difficult life experiences. "Dirty pain" is the damaging, multiplied pain we create when we catastrophize, judge ourselves, or allow ourselves to be judged by others. Dirty pain is the story we tell ourselves about the clean pain. Dirty pain is the imaginary obstacles we put in our own way.

We can banish imaginary obstacles by poking at them, though. Instead of continuing to speculate or assuming, we can find out the truth. We can ask. We can discuss. When we poke our dirty fears, they often pop and vanish.

Today I'm going to talk to someone about something that's been bothering me. I'm going to find out if it's real or imaginary, clean pain or dirty pain. Either way, talking about it will be an amazing relief.

JUNE 24

"The world is a book, and those who do not travel read only a page."
— Saint Augustine

Traveling while in deep grief is not the same experience as traveling at other times. We should not fool ourselves into thinking that we can leave our grief behind and "have fun." No, our grief lives inside us, and we take it with us wherever we go.

But travel can sometimes help us on our journey through grief. Going somewhere picturesque and peaceful can provide a healing backdrop in which to embrace our pain. A new locale can also help us see things with a new perspective. What's more, other cultures handle grief and loss differently. We might meet new people who turn out to be transformative companions in our journey.

We needn't go somewhere exotic or far-flung, though, to reap the benefits of travel. If our budgets or time are tight, we can simply visit places in our own communities we have never been before, or take a drive an hour or two away. The point is to take our grief somewhere new and see what the motion of travel can do to help us embrace and soften it.

I think I'll take my grief somewhere it's never been today.

JUNE 25

"You are loved, and your purpose is to love."
— Marianne Williamson

In grief we realize that this is the catch-22 of life.

Love is the most joyous and meaningful experience there is.
Love gives our lives purpose. But love's conjoined twin is grief.
If we love, we will eventually grieve.

So what is there to do but continue loving? When we express
our ongoing love for the person who died, we are mourning
and moving toward healing. When we embrace the love of
others, we are accepting the balm of grace and healing. If we
shun or hide ourselves from love, on the other hand,
we are choosing to die while we are alive.

Love, then, is not just the best answer—it is the only answer.

At every turn, I will try to remember that I am loved and
that I am here to love. If I let love guide me,
I will find my way to hope and healing.

JUNE 26

*"Of the widow's countless death-duties, there is really just one that
matters: on the first anniversary of her husband's death,
the widow should think, 'I kept myself alive.'"*

— Joyce Carol Oates

The anniversary of the death can be so hard. We think about the
day the person died—where we were, how it happened, how
we found out, how we reacted, how others reacted. We can't
help but relive the experience that so devastated our lives.

Instead of trying to "just keep busy" on the anniversary of the
death, maybe it would be better for us to honor it as a day of
remembrance. We could take the day off work, cancel other
commitments, and forgo mundane tasks. We can visit the grave
or scattering site, look through photo albums, and spend the
day in the company of others who miss our special person.

It's a good day for ritual. Creating an anniversary-date ritual
gives us a structure for getting through the day. We can include
poems, prayers, music, and other elements of ceremony
if we'd like. Ritual has the power to transform chaos into
transcendence. And especially in the early anniversary years, we
can also simply appreciate the fact that we kept ourselves alive.

*I can choose to honor the anniversary of the death
and give it the time, attention, and structure befitting my love
for the person who died.*

JUNE 27

"Learn to say 'no' to the good so you can say 'yes' to the best."
— John C. Maxwell

To create time and space for grief and mourning, we often have to pare back. We need to offload commitments we no longer have the energy for. We have to clear our schedules of good-but-not-critical optional activities.

Right now, saying 'yes' to the best means saying 'yes' to mourning…because saying 'yes' to mourning is actually saying 'yes' to healing. It also means saying 'yes' to others when they want to connect and support us. And it means saying 'yes' to our children or others who need our presence and support. We need ample free time for all of these things.

Eventually we find that saying 'yes' to mourning and good grief support leads to being ready to say 'yes' to other people and activities we love or find meaningful. We say 'yes' to grief today so that eventually we can wholeheartedly say 'yes' to life again.

I can say 'no' whenever I need to in order to say 'yes' to grief, mourning, and healing.

JUNE 28

"If you cannot see where you are going, ask someone who has been there before."

— J. Loren Norris

Millions of other grievers have walked this path before us. I've spoken with lots of them along the way. They want to let us know that we can and will survive this. We can't always see where we're going, but they've been there, and they know.

Sometimes it helps to have a grief mentor with whom we can meet and talk face-to-face. A person who has experienced a loss similar to ours is a good candidate, though more important than the particulars of the loss may be the griever's attitude, sense of hopefulness, and willingness to help. (However, we should also be careful not to pair ourselves with someone who believes that grief and mourning must be done *his way*. A grief mentor should be a companion and example more than a teacher.)

I myself have turned to grief mentors at certain challenging, grief-overloaded moments during my career as a grief counselor. Everyone needs one-on-one help sometimes. It's nothing to be ashamed of.

When I can't see where I'm going, I can ask someone who's been there before.

JUNE 29

"Be not afraid of going slowly; be afraid only of standing still."
— Chinese proverb

Our culture wants us to hurry up and get over it already. In this age of instant gratification, we are expected to start feeling better the week after the funeral. C'mon! Chop-chop!

In other arenas of our lives, though, we're learning to appreciate anew the slow pleasures, such as slow food (thoughtfully grown, locally sourced, and cooked from scratch); slow coffee (pour-over and cold brew); and slow parenting (no overbooked activity schedules, just simple time together).

Earlier this year I began to advocate for something I'm calling "slow grief." The slow grief movement acknowledges that loss is as much a part of the human experience as love. It recognizes that loss changes us forever and that grief is a normal, necessary, and, yes, sssllllooowwww process. It also proclaims the need for people to express their grief and to be supported by their communities. And it asks us to look to the past to recapture the healing wisdom and customs we have almost lost (such as multiday funerals).

Grief is slow. We mustn't be afraid of its slowness. We mustn't try to rush it. As long as we're putting our grief into motion through active mourning, we're not standing still.
And that's all that matters.

I'm not afraid of going slowly in grief.
Healing is a naturally slow process.

JUNE 30

*"There is no exercise better for the heart than reaching down
and lifting people up."*

— John Holmes

As grievers, we need the help and support of others. But
somewhere along the way we will also be ready and able to
give help and support to fellow travelers.

The more we actively mourn and explore what truly helps us
heal, the more equipped we become to help others. And
the more we help others, the more we heal.

When we feel ready, we can look for opportunities to be grief
companions. Our new, hard-won awareness and understanding
of grief and mourning should be gently shared. We can help
transform our culture into one that embraces normal,
necessary grief instead of avoids it.

*If I am ready, I will reach out to help someone
else who is grieving. I now know that a simple note,
phone call, or conversation can mean so much.*

JULY 1

*"Anything that's human is mentionable, and anything that is
mentionable can be more manageable. When we can talk about our
feelings, they become less overwhelming, less upsetting, and less scary.
The people we trust with that important talk can help us
know that we are not alone."*

— Fred Rogers

Many of us were raised in families and cultures in which death
and grief were not openly discussed. If we were hurting, we
were met with unspoken and spoken rules such as "suck it up,"
"keep our chins up," and "move on."

But Mr. Rogers is right. Anything that's human is mentionable,
and what is more human than the grief that follows loss?

Grief is normal and necessary. And talking about it with others,
which is perhaps the most fundamental way to mourn, makes it
less overwhelming, less upsetting, and less scary. So anytime
we want to feel less overwhelmed, upset, and scared,
let's remember to mention away.

*I will mention my grief. I will find others who are good at
listening and empathizing without judgment, and I will trust
them with my important talk.*

JULY 2

"Don't assume, ask. Be kind. Tell the truth. Don't say anything you can't stand behind fully. Have integrity. Tell people how you feel."

— Warsan Shire

If we hear "I know how you feel" one more time, we might lose it. "Did you live my exact life?" we want to ask the people who tell us this. "Did you have the exact same relationship and experiences? Precisely the same loss?"

I don't presume to know exactly how *you* feel, dear reader. I know we likely have had many similar thoughts, feelings, and experiences during our grief journeys. And I appreciate the affirmation and understanding we can give each other. But to truly empathize with you on any given day, I can't assume. I must ask. And when I ask, I am hoping you will tell me the truth about how and what you are feeling.

Let's have grace for all those "I know how you feel"ers out there, because they are no doubt trying to let us know that they have empathy for us, but let's also do our part by telling the truth about how we are feeling.

The only way for others to know what I am thinking and feeling is for me to tell them.

JULY 3

"Do you have the patience to wait till your mud settles and the
water is clear? Can you remain unmoving till the
right action arises by itself?"

— Lao Tzu

Our mud is still settling, that's for sure.
Everything is murky and unclear.

We do not like the mud and murkiness. We want out! But we're
discovering: If we keep flailing about, we only stir up more
mud. Our frantic, mindless attempts to keep busy and
get things sorted out quickly are just muddying
our waters even more.

What would happen if we were patiently still? If we withdrew
into ourselves and tried to remain unmoving and calm for a
while? Maybe our waters would clear. Perhaps our next
right action would arise by itself.

When my waters are muddy, I will try stilling myself and
patiently waiting for them to clear.

JULY 4

"I am no bird, and no net ensnares me.
I am a free human being with an independent will."
— Charlotte Brontë

Grief makes clear our interdependence with others, and it is this interdependence that gives our lives joy and meaning. And yet the paradox is that each of us is a singular human being with an independent will and consciousness.

What this means is that our grief is unique. The thoughts, feelings, and memories we harbor inside us aren't quite like anyone else's. It also means that our most effective methods of mourning are unique. What works for me might not work for you, and vice versa. In this way, our grief and mourning are independent.

And yet, the healing of our independent grief is dependent, in part, on the support and compassion of others. Such is the mystery of love, grief, and life.

I am both independent and dependent in my grief.
Healing requires both.

JULY 5

"The doors we open and close each day decide the lives we live."
— Flora Whittemore

A door got closed on us, and we didn't like it. Sometimes we're not in charge of which doors get opened and which get closed. That can make life feel unfair and painful.

But sometimes we *are* in charge of openings and closings. When it comes to our grief, we have the option of moving toward our thoughts and feelings. If we feel guilt or regret inside, for example, it's like we have a door labeled "guilt." We can choose to approach the door and open it, or we can choose to continue to walk by it, knowing it's there (and suffering the pain of it) yet avoiding examining it and working through it.

In grief we can also choose to close some doors if and when we're ready. We can distance ourselves from people who are shaming us about our natural and necessary grief. After opening a door to a particular thought or feeling, we can sometimes end up closing it behind us for good because we've reconciled it. We can also learn to close the door on cultural misconceptions about grief and mourning.

**The grief doors I open and close each day
determine my path to healing.**

JULY 6

*"I was never insane, except upon occasion
when my heart was touched."*

— Edgar Allen Poe

Grief can feel a lot like going crazy. We find ourselves in a new
reality, where everything we thought was up is down and vice
versa. Our thinking is jumbled. Our feelings fly all over
the place. Our every routine is discombobulated.

It can help to remind ourselves that we're not actually going
crazy. We're grieving. Our hearts have been touched—shattered,
actually—by loss, and our lives have fallen to the ground in
a million pieces. No wonder everything seems so
disjointed and messy.

We can remind ourselves that abnormal is the new normal
for now, and that's normal.

***When I feel like I'm going crazy, I can stop, breathe deeply, and
remember that it's just my normal and necessary grief.***

JULY 7

"There are no shortcuts to any place worth going."
— Beverly Sills

Months in to the most significant personal griefs I have
experienced, I've found myself looking around and thinking,
"This journey is too long and too hard. Where
are the shortcuts?"

Of course, there are no shortcuts to healing in grief. It takes
a great deal of time and lots of effort. It takes embracing and
expressing all the thoughts and feelings as they come along.
It takes work. The only way out is through.

But reconciliation of our grief is indeed a destination worth
working toward. Healing allows us to live and love fully again.

There are no shortcuts in grief. The only way out is through.

JULY 8

"Without you in my arms, I feel an emptiness in my soul. I find myself searching the crowds for your face. I know it's an impossibility, but I cannot help myself."

—Nicholas Sparks

It's natural to search for our loved ones who have died. We can't help ourselves. Our minds and hearts can't accept that they are really gone, so we look for them. And even when we're not actively keeping an eye out for them, we sometimes spot them—a glimpse of a cheek, a set of shoulders in the distance, a fall of hair from behind, a face in a car whizzing by.

Our searching and yearning are part of our grief. We so very much want our special loved ones right here next to us. When we catch a glimpse of someone who reminds us of the person who died, it's OK to follow our impulse to approach for a closer look. Sometimes our minds are only satisfied by what our eyes can see.

Over time, as our hearts come to fully embrace the reality, we will search less and remember more

I am searching for you. I am yearning for you.
When I see someone who reminds me of you,
I will send that person a silent blessing.

JULY 9

"Mistakes are the usual bridge between inexperience and wisdom."
— Phyllis Theroux

We all make plenty of mistakes in life. That's how we learn.

How to grieve and mourn in ways that lead to healing also takes learning, especially in a culture that gets it backward. So we're likely to make mistakes along the way. We might keep things bottled up inside, or we might turn to alcohol, drugs, or other addictive behaviors in an attempt to dull our pain. Some of us try to distract ourselves from our grief by keeping overly busy. Others of us take care of other people but don't take care of ourselves.

When we make mistakes in our grief journeys, we can chalk them up to inexperience and cultural misconceptions and try again. I've found that wisdom in grief and mourning usually comes slowly. So let's be patient and self-forgiving.

If I make mistakes during my grief journey, that just means I am learning and accruing wisdom.

JULY 10

"Do I contradict myself?
Very well then,
I contradict myself.
I am large.
I contain multitudes."

— Walt Whitman

We grievers contain multitudes. We've got an awful lot of thoughts, feelings, and memories roiling around us. We might behave in ways that seem weird or out of character.

Sometimes our thoughts, feelings, and behaviors might contradict one another. Very well then, we contradict ourselves…and that's OK. We're figuring things out. We're works in progress.

I contain multitudes. I'm plenty large enough to contain all my inner realities, and when I express them, I'm giving them more room to roam.

JULY 11

"Here I am, where I ought to be."
— Louise Erdrich

We are right where we need to be in our grief journeys.
Whatever we're thinking and feeling is exactly what we
need to be thinking and feeling.

We often question if we're "normal." We wonder if it's normal to
have a certain thought or feel a certain feeling. We wonder if
it's normal for grief to last as long as it's lasting.

Rest assured, we're normal. You're normal, and I'm normal
(if there is such a thing as normal). Given our unique
circumstances, histories, and personalities, we're right where we
ought to be. If we're feeling stuck or in despair, we only need
remember that active mourning will get us going again.

Where I am today is right where I ought to be.

JULY 12

"The growth of understanding follows an ascending spiral rather than a straight line."

— Joanna Field

At the beginning of our first great grief, we might have faith that things will only get better. Yes, it hurts so much we're not sure we can survive, but surely each day the pain will lessen until it eventually doesn't hurt anymore…right?

And then we figure out that the pain gets worse before it gets better. Not only that, we learn that there's no straight line to healing. It's more like wandering around in the dark.

When I feel like I'm getting lost in the darkness of my grief, I sometimes conjure this image of the spiral. A spiral is constantly doubling back on itself, covering the same territory, but it's also, at the same time, ascending. It's going up. It's reaching new heights. As we climb the mountain of our grief, we're hiking the spiraling path that takes us to the summit. It's strenuous and rocky, and we're tired. And while the trail sometime dips downward for a stretch in keeping with the terrain, it eventually, and overall, goes up.

My grief does not follow a straight line to healing, but as it twists and turns, it does ascend.

JULY 13

"Everyone at some point will suffer a loss—the loss of loved ones, good health, a job. It's your desert experience—a time of feeling barren of options, even hope. The important thing is not to allow yourself to be stranded in the desert."

— Patrick Del Zoppo

I have a home in the desert of Arizona. It can be a severe and dangerous place. It is barren of foliage and water. The sun scorches. The wind howls. There is nowhere to hide.

Our grief can feel like this—malevolent and unrelenting. But in my desert, as in the desert of our grief, there is also startling beauty. If I look closely, I will see tiny blooms where I thought there was nothing but barrenness. I will see the grandeur of the rock formations. I will notice the piercing blueness of the sky.

Yes, grief is a desert experience. It is a life-threatening journey, for if we do not actively mourn, we may be forever stranded there, dying while we are alive. Thank goodness for mourning. It brings us safely through.

In the desert of my grief, I will be on the watch for bits of beauty. I will also keep moving by expressing my grief, for to stop for too long in the desert is to die while I am alive.

JULY 14

"Faith is the bird that feels the light when the dawn is still dark."
— Rabindranath Tagore

Some among us have religious or spiritual faith. We believe that God or a benevolent greater power is taking care of us, and no matter what happens here on earth, all is actually well. We trust that somehow, some way, our souls will enjoy immortality and be reunited with the souls of those who have passed before us. Such faith offers us profound comfort during our time of grief.

Others among us do not have such faith, and we are struggling to find reasons to get our feet out of bed in the morning. I'd like us to consider that the concept of "faith" need not only be religious. In grief, we can have faith that we will have new opportunities to laugh and love. That we can still be surprised and awed. That our grief will soften.

Faith is a belief not based on proof or concrete evidence. We do not have proof about what tomorrow will bring, but we can choose to believe—today—that good things are coming.

I have faith that _____.
Nurturing my faith in my most fundamental beliefs—
whatever they are—will help me heal.

JULY 15

"Man never made any material as resilient as the human spirit."
— Bernard Williams

Since the death, we may have been encouraged to "bounce back," "move past it," or "get over it." But we know now that's not how grief works. Grief takes time and energy. It's a slog of hard, painful work. How ridiculous to think that the death of a loved one is something we could ever simply and quickly "get over."

At the same time, we are more resilient than we sometimes give ourselves credit for. If we mourn actively and thoroughly for as long as we need to, we *will* bounce back. It's just more of a slow-motion bounce.

Imagine a tennis ball. The whack of the racquet (like the death) sends it careening onto the court floor. Can you picture it in extra-slow-mo, spinning downward, downward, downward? Finally it hits the court. It has reached bottom. But wait! No, it hasn't. In this one-frame-at-a-time view, we can see the ball flatten against the ground. The impact crushes it. Only after plummeting and being almost destroyed does it begin to regain its form and gather the momentum to slowly, slowly, slowly bounce skyward again.

I am crushed, but I also have faith in my resilience.

JULY 16

"It has been a terrible, horrible, no good, very bad day.
My mom says some days are like that."

— Judith Viorst

Some days in grief are just plain bad. We feel sad, hopeless, afraid, or alone. We can't seem to escape the despair, even for a few minutes. Then sometimes even more bad things happen, compounding grief upon grief.

We can always try venting about our bad days to someone who cares about us. We can also try writing in a journal, meditating, or attending a support group. All of these activities can help, but some days, nothing seems to break through the clouds.

When we are grief overloaded or grief-sodden, sometimes the best thing to do is call it a day. We can turn off our phones, put on our pajamas, and crawl into bed. If we're not sleepy, we can do something that reliably distracts us, such as binge-watching TV, losing ourselves in a novel, or taking a long bath. We can do something effective (but harmless) to get us through this terrible, horrible, no good, very bad day, trusting that tomorrow will be better.

The next time I have a really bad day, I will give myself a
much-needed break and do something that soothes me—
anything that gets me safely through until tomorrow.

JULY 17

"But here I am in July, and why am I thinking about Christmas pudding? Probably because we always pine for what we do not have. The winter seems cozy and romantic in the hell of summer, but hot beaches and sunlight are what we yearn for all winter."

— Joanna Franklin Bell

That about sums up our grief: We are pining for what we do not have. Yet when we had our special people with us, we did not always appreciate the moments we shared.

Such is human nature. It's all but impossible to constantly live in appreciation of the now. We're equipped with minds that remember as well as project into the future. Through our imagination, we travel through time and space at the drop of a hat. This is both a gift and a curse.

But maintaining a mindful presence is something we can work on. The more skilled at it we become, the more we are likely to appreciate the rest of our days. We will always remember (thank goodness) and worry about what is to come, but we can also become more adept at inhabiting the now.

I am pining for what I do not have—you.
I am working on appreciating what I do have right now.

JULY 18

"Most people don't know how brave they really are."
— R.E. Chambers

Everyone grieves, but it takes courage to mourn. To express what we're thinking and feeling inside. To open up and lay ourselves bare. To expose our most tender inner truths to the harsh world.

In grief, as in most things, bravery begets more bravery. We find that if we muster the courage, finally, to tell a friend a hard truth about our grief, we have more courage for the next mourning opportunity. That's because usually our courage is rewarded. We put ourselves out there, and in doing so we notice that others offer empathy and support. We also feel a sense of relief and release just from having unburdened ourselves for the moment.

In grief, bravery can foster healing.

I am braver than I think. I can marshal my courage to help myself heal.

JULY 19

*"Grief is like the ocean; it comes on waves, ebbing and flowing.
Sometimes the water is calm, and sometimes it is overwhelming.
All you can do is learn to swim."*

— Vicki Harrison

Grief is as unpredictable as the ocean. It is also as vast and as
deep and as powerful. We cannot fight it or control it.
We can only surrender to it.

When we learn to swim in our grief, we adjust our speed and
direction based on the current conditions. We can only
go where the waves allow us to go.

Sometimes we go nowhere. On those days, all we can do
is float and survive.

Just as we respect the ocean, we will respect our grief.

*I will swim in the ocean of my grief,
allowing it to determine my path and speed.*

JULY 20

"In the midst of winter, I found there was, within me, an invincible summer. And that makes me happy. For it says that no matter how hard the world pushes against me, within me, there's something stronger—something better, pushing right back."

— Albert Camus

I, too, believe that there is something invincible within all of us. It is our soul, lit by our divine spark.

Our divine sparks are the embers of meaning and purpose that live within us. We were born; therefore we live; therefore we have a right and reason to be here. Our grief naturally subdues our divine sparks, but they still glimmer deep down inside. We just have to find and feed the flame, though that's not easy to do sometimes.

We descend into our grief so that, like the phoenix, we can rise and transcend. And all the while our invincible divine sparks glow within us, lighting the way.

There is within me an invincible summer.

JULY 21

"Be careful how you are talking to yourself because you are listening."
— Lisa M. Hayes

When we are grieving, our self-talk can be self-defeating.

"I'm not strong enough to mourn and heal."
"I can't live without _____."
"I didn't do everything I could have. I'm a terrible person."
"I'm such a mess! Why am I so incapable?"
"I'm never going to be happy again."

It's understandable, the way we sometimes talk to ourselves.
We're broken, yet we live in a culture that sees grief
as illness and mourning as weakness.

We can't change the death. But we *can* change how we talk to
ourselves about it. When we catch ourselves in self-defeating
self-talk, let's try these much truer affirmations instead.

"I possess all the strength and grace I need to mourn and heal."
"I can live without _____, though I will always miss him/her."
"To be human is to make mistakes. I am a glorious
expression of humanity."
"I'm grieving, and grieving is messy but also good."
"I will do my grief work so that I can be happy again."

***I will work on talking to myself in positive,
self-compassionate ways.***

JULY 22

"Lots of people want to ride with you in the limo, but what you want is someone who will take the bus with you when the limo breaks down."

— Oprah Winfrey

Turns out that quite a few of our friends were of the fair-weather variety. When the going got tough, they got going.

Our culture doesn't teach people how to be present to grief, so it's no wonder that so few of our friends and family members have stuck around.

But still, we need people to listen to us and support us in our grief. We can't do it alone! I guess we should be grateful for the handful of people who have climbed onto the bus with us and are willing to go along for the ride. Thank you, true friends.

I understand why so few people seem to be able to support me in my grief, and I am grateful for those precious few who can.

JULY 23

"All emotions, even those that are suppressed and unexpressed, have physical effects. Unexpressed emotions tend to stay in the body like small ticking time bombs—they are illnesses in incubation."

— Marilyn Van Derbur

Our grief hurts us physically. Our bodies ache.
We might feel ill or simply "not right."

It's no wonder. We are missing a physical presence—one our bodies knew and loved. What's more, stress hormones continue to cascade through our systems, and their lingering presence makes us feel unwell.

Besides taking care of ourselves physically, which is so important right now, the main way in which we can heal our bodies is to work on healing our hearts and souls. If we continue to work at actively expressing our grief, our stress hormones will dissipate, our souls will unclench, and our bodies will find relief.

Caring for my heart and soul also helps my body feel better.

JULY 24

"It has been said that there are several ways to mourn. One is to weep; and we have done our share of weeping. Another way to mourn is to sing: to sing a hymn to life, a life that still abounds in sights and sounds and vivid colors; to sing the song our beloved no longer has the chance to sing. We sing the songs of our beloved; we aspire to their qualities of spirit; we take up their tasks as they would have shouldered them."

— Rabbi Jack Stern, Jr.

As my embarrassed children can attest, I have been known to crank up the music and belt out Frank Sinatra songs at the top of my lungs. Singing is fun! Like dancing, it's a way to let the healing power of music connect with our souls.

But here Rabbi Stern is talking about more than actual singing. He's saying we should live boldly and passionately in ways that the people who died would have. We can choose to sing their songs. We can finish some of their tasks and carry out some of their passions. My dad loved Frank Sinatra. Whenever I sing his songs, I'm singing for Dad.

We sing with our voices, and we sing with our spirits. Both are outlets and balms for our grief.

The person who died had a song to sing.
I'm going to keep singing it for him.

JULY 25

"Nothing ever goes away until it teaches us what we need to know."
— Pema Chodron

Our grief has so much to teach us that it's never going to go away—at least not completely. But if we become its devoted students, listening and fully attending, it will slowly relinquish the lectern. Eventually it will step away and stand benevolently in the background.

While our grief is still our daily master, let's acknowledge and pay attention to it. It is teaching us things we need to know—perhaps the most important things there *are* to know, actually.

My grief is teaching me things I need to know.
I will be a devoted student.

JULY 26

"Wounds don't heal the way you want them to; they heal the way they need to. It takes time for wounds to fade into scars. It takes time for the process of healing to take place. Give yourself that time. Give yourself that grace. Be gentle with your wounds. Be gentle with your heart. You deserve to heal."

— Dele Olanubi

Yes, it takes time and, most important, the process of active mourning for healing to unfold. We must be patient and give ourselves that time. We must give ourselves the grace of reaching out for and accepting the support of others. Along the way, we must be gentle with ourselves and our wounded hearts.

But we must also and always hold onto this thought: We deserve to heal. This is a statement of our intention to heal. It is a declaration of hope.

We deserve to heal. We deserve to live and love fully again. We deserve to experience meaning for the rest of our days. As singular souls, as children of God, as the people entrusted to carry on the precious legacies of those who have died, it is our right and our destiny and our purpose to shine again.

I deserve the gentleness, time, and attention to mourning I need to heal. I do deserve to heal.

JULY 27

"Your task is not to seek for love, but merely to seek and find all the barriers within yourself that you have built against it."

— Rumi

Because love and grief are two sides of the same precious coin, the barriers we build for one are also barriers to the other. We're here together on this page, though, because we did let love in. And now we must drop any barriers we may have erected to letting our resulting grief out.

For example, have we built walls to hold in our tears? Crying is good for us in grief. It's time to knock down those walls if they exist. Likewise barriers to accepting help from others. When people reach out to us, do we tell them we're fine and send them away? If so, let's take a sledgehammer to those walls and let the compassion and empathy of others in.

Whenever our grief is knocking at our soul's door, let us also seek out and find all the barriers within ourselves that we may have built against it. Just as love was our true purpose, so now is our grief.

I will seek out and find any barriers I may have built within myself to honestly and fully acknowledging and sharing my grief.

JULY 28

*"The trick is to be grateful when your mood is high
and graceful when it is low."*
— Richard Carlson

Even in our grief, our moods are sometimes high. We
experience lightness, laughter, and joy. Thank goodness.
The darkness would be too much without these moments of
reprieve. Let's remember to notice and be grateful for them.

When our moods are low, on the other hand, we must find the
grace to befriend them. They can feel like the homeless person
on the corner—something ragged and messy, something we
would rather avert our eyes from and pretend is not there. But
if we stop and bear witness to them, if we extend them our
kindness and compassion, if we sit with them and get to know
them, we will see that they are us. And we are them.

That is grace.

*May I be grateful when my mood is high
and graceful when it is low.*

JULY 29

"Anger is just anger. It isn't good. It isn't bad. It just is. What you do with it is what matters. It's like anything else. You can use it to build or to destroy. You just have to make a choice."

— Jim Butcher

Many of us were raised to believe that anger is one of the bad emotions. But really, it's got just as much a right to show up as happiness, sadness, fear, or any other feeling.

When we're feeling angry in grief, it tends to make other people uncomfortable. After all, anger can be assertive and loud. It can even be violent.

While our anger isn't good or bad, what we do with it is what matters. We can use it to build or destroy. We can express and explore our anger by talking to others who care about us—not blaming or raging. If we feel the need to use our bodies to express our anger, we can turn to physical activities like sports or making art. We can choose to use our anger to build relationships, physical wellness, and self-understanding.

My anger needs constructive outlets.

JULY 30

*"Softness is not weakness. It takes courage to stay delicate
in a world this cruel."*

— Beau Taplin

We are hurting because we understand the necessity of
delicateness. Without a soft, delicate heart, we could not love.
Yet it is this same soft, delicate heart that now grieves.

Our softness makes us vulnerable to this often-cruel world,
it's true. But at the same time, it's the only thing that
makes life worth living.

Our softness is our strength. Our delicateness is our opportunity
to heal and grow, laugh and love, and live fully
the rest of our days.

*My heart is soft and delicate.
It is the source of my hurt but also my healing.*

JULY 31

"Spirituality leaps where science cannot yet follow, because science must always test and measure, and much of reality and human experience is immeasurable."

— Starhawk

In other books, magazine articles, and websites, you might run across a philosophy (and even "studies") that claims that humans are resilient and do not need to express their grief or receive support for it. The "new science of grief," as it is sometimes called, essentially claims that people "get over" grief on their own, over time, and that grief naturally heals itself.

But scientific findings can't really measure a soul-based experience. What's more, scientific research on grief may well end up falsely affirming, because of confirmation bias, our culture's tendency to avoid grief instead of befriending it.

We *do* need to mourn our grief to heal it, and we *do* need and deserve the love and care of others along the way, including, at times, the lifeline of a grief support group and the companionship of a skilled grief counselor. To mourn is to find our way back to a life of joy and love.

My grief is a spiritual journey of the heart and soul. I will remember this if others try to "science" my grief.

AUGUST 1

*"One thing: you have to walk, and create the way by your walking;
you will not find a ready-made path. It is not so cheap, to reach to the
ultimate realization of truth. You will have to create the path by
walking yourself; the path is not ready-made, lying there and waiting
for you. It is just like the sky: the birds fly, but they don't
leave any footprints. You cannot follow them;
there are no footprints left behind."*

— Osho

Each of us has to create our own path through the wilderness
of our grief. Though others have gone before us, they inhabited
their own unique wilderness; they created
their own unique path.

We have to walk; we create the way by our own walking.

And so we look ahead, seeing no clear path. We only know we
need to move. So we take a step. And that step helps us
know when and how to take another.

***I will create my path through grief by discovering
and walking it myself.***

AUGUST 2

"Faith and doubt are both needed—not as antagonists but working side by side—to take us around the unknown curve."

— Lillian Smith

Sometimes we mistakenly believe that we either have faith or we don't. It's actually almost never such a black-and-white, either-or duality.

I have found that even the people with the strongest faith wrestle with doubts. Questioning God is OK. He can handle it.

Conversely, I've also noticed that people who profess to have no faith often wonder, question, and slip in and out of some form of belief. Agnostics believe that we can't know; they neither believe nor disbelieve. In this way, they are like tightrope walkers, holding out one arm into each realm for balance.

Faith and doubt are complementary. Most of us will lean on both of them as they take us around the unknown curve.

My doubt and my faith are both normal and necessary.
Regardless of the proportions I hold, I can trust that
the mixture will take me around the unknown curve.

AUGUST 3

"Summer is the annual permission slip to be lazy. To do nothing and have it count for something. To lie in the grass and count the stars. To sit on a branch and study the clouds."

— Regina Brett

Here in America we have a cultural bias against laziness. We are a country of doers instead of be-ers. We have bought into the fallacy that unless we are "doing something," we are wasting time.

Yet grief reminds us of the necessity of nothing-doing. Our grief slows us down and makes us lethargic. Like the heat of August, it depletes our energy. It makes us lazy. And in the lassitude of grief, we do the necessary work of thinking our thoughts and feeling our feelings.

Our inertia is essential to our healing.

When I am feeling lazy, I will recognize the necessity of doing nothing. I am learning to embrace laziness and just be.

AUGUST 4

*"Life is a shipwreck, but we must not forget
to sing in the lifeboats."*

—Voltaire

Life is a shipwreck; terrible tragedies happen all the time, most notably the deaths of people we love. Alas, this is so very true.

But! There are lifeboats. There are people and experiences that can save us from sinking along with the wreckage. There is help for our profound grief.

And! Once we're in the lifeboats, we cannot only cry—we can sing. After we've been rescued from drowning in our grief and we're bobbing in our lifeboat—still traumatized but relatively safe and warm—we can choose to celebrate the fact that we and the others in the lifeboat are still alive.

We acknowledge and embrace the loss, and then we learn to celebrate what remains.

*My life may be a shipwreck,
but I can choose to sing in the lifeboat.*

AUGUST 5

"In time, in time they tell me, I'll not feel so bad. I don't want time to heal me. There's a reason I'm like this. I want time to set me ugly and knotted with loss of you, marking me. I won't smooth you away. I can't say goodbye."

— China Miéville

Sometimes we think that healing our grief means letting go of the person who died. We feel guilty for laughing or having fun. We feel ambivalent about getting rid of possessions or taking on a new challenge of our own. We want to hang onto our grief as a way of hanging onto our loyalty to the person who died.

We don't have to try to hang onto our grief, though. It has marked us. It's part of who we are. We can't move on without it any more than we could move on without our elbows and noses.

Yet at the same time, we also don't really have to say goodbye. The love goes on. The relationship of memory goes on. We continue on—branded by our grief but healing, saying hello to our futures without ever saying goodbye to our pasts.

I want to remember you and to keep healing. I want to honor you always and say hello to my future.

AUGUST 6

"Fair's in August."
— Midwestern Saying

Life is Not Fair.

While someone we love died, so many other people still live.
Our special person was too young/healthy/precious/needed/
careful/good to die! Why him or her? Why us?

In the midwestern United States, where I grew up, adults had
a wise rejoinder to the common children's complaint, "That's
not fair!" "Fair's in August," the grown-ups would say. You see,
the county and state fairs always took place in August. "Fair's in
August" was a way of saying that there *was* no such thing
as fair—at least not the kind of fair we kids meant.

It's true. Life isn't fair. From our vantage point, people die who
should live, and people live who maybe shouldn't. And some
people have to bear more than their fair share of loss. The only
thing we can do in the face of all this unfairness is to help each
other through it. A slice of blue-ribbon pie never hurts, either.

I need to talk about the unfairness today.
Talking helps rounds off its sharp edges.

AUGUST 7

"There are no wrong turnings—only paths we had not known we were meant to walk."

— Guy Gavriel Kay

Our lives weren't supposed to turn out like this. Oh sure—people have to die, but not *these* people! Not now! Not in this way!

We might believe that life took a wrong turn on us, and it's normal and necessary to get upset and vent when that happens. But eventually, after all the venting is done, we sometimes reach a new understanding. Maybe life didn't take a wrong turn on us. Maybe it took a path we had not thought we were meant to walk.

So here we are on this new path. It's different from our old path. We will always miss the old path, but maybe, if we give it a chance, we will find that the new path takes us to people and places filled with meaning and joy.

I am on a path I had not known I was meant to walk.
I am learning to give the new path a chance.

AUGUST 8

"If you're happy in a dream, does that count?"
— Arundhati Roy

Sometimes we can't stop thinking about the death—
even in our sleep. We dream about the person who died.

Dreams are one of the ways the work of mourning takes place.
A dream may reflect a searching for the person who has died,
for example. We may dream that we are with the person in a
crowded place and lose him and cannot find him. Dreams also
provide opportunities—to feel happy and close to the person
who died, to embrace the reality of the death, to gently confront
the depth of the loss, to renew memories, or to develop a new
self-identity. Dreams also may help us search for meaning in life
and death or explore unfinished business. Finally, dreams
can show us hope for the future.

Dreaming about the person who died is normal and natural. It's
also helpful, because it's a form of mourning. Nightmares about
the person who died, on the other hand, are frightening and
distressing, even if they, too, are working out our thoughts and
feelings. If you're having nightmares, be sure to talk about
them with a good friend or counselor.

*My happy dreams about the person who died help express
my continuing love. They count.*

AUGUST 9

*"Look on each day that comes as a challenge, as a test of courage.
The pain will come in waves, some days worse than others, for no
apparent reason. Accept the pain. Little by little, you will find new
strength, new vision, born of the very pain and loneliness
which seem, at first, impossible to master."*

— Daphne du Maurier

When we are in grief, every day is a challenge. We must find
the strength to get out of bed, dress and feed ourselves, and go
out into the world and interact with others. We must summon
the fortitude to do what needs to be done even though we are
so heartbroken inside. And through it all we must muster
the courage to encounter and embrace our pain.

That's a lot of heavy lifting. But over time, the heavy lifting
gives us more strength and more courage. It's not unlike
weight lifting, actually. We start by hoisting small weights,
and even so, our muscles get sore. It's hard. Slowly but surely,
though, if we keep at it, we are able to lift heavier and heavier
weights, and in the process we grow healthier and more
capable. Months later, we're changed people.

So it is with grief. If we take each day as a challenge and we
commit to mourning, we grow stronger and more capable.
Months later, we're changed people—people who eventually
are able to live and love fully again.

*I accept the challenge of today. I will find the courage not only to
survive but to embrace and express my thoughts and feelings
about the death as they arise.*

AUGUST 10

"Mortals. Everything is so black and white to you."
— Kami Garcia

We tend to compartmentalize things as either/or. Happy or sad.
Good or bad. That's because we as a culture aren't comfortable
with ambiguity. We prefer clear-cut truths, answers,
and states of being.

But our grief is every shade of gray. We're not happy or sad.
We're happy *and* sad. We're also afraid and mad and confused
and tired and hopeful. Notice all those "and"s? Like life itself,
grief is all of those things and more.

When we're feeling a certain painful emotion or thinking a
certain challenging thought, let's remember the power of *and*.
We can be torn apart *and* enjoying the company of friends. We
can be lonely *and* grateful *and* disorganized, all in the same
moment. We are complex creatures living in a complex world.
We are not one thing or another. We're everything all at once.
Ambiguity and chaos rein.

Everything belongs.

My grief is not black or white.
It is every shade of gray all at once.

AUGUST 11

"Everyone must believe in something. I believe I'll go canoeing."
— Henry David Thoreau

Most of us question our beliefs after the death of someone loved. Grief is a time of searching for meaning in life and death.

Whether or not we have something we call "faith," we all have beliefs. For example, I believe that if you do good work, good things will happen. I believe that spending time in nature is healing. I believe that singing and humor are good for you. I also believe in openness, kindness, and the transformative power of mourning.

What do *you* believe? What are the beliefs that form the foundation of your life and give you a reason to get out of bed in the morning? Spiritual guru Deepak Chopra recommends cultivating the following four foundational beliefs: I am loved; I am worthy; I am safe; and I am whole.

When we're in the painful process of questioning our foundational beliefs, though, sometimes we might need to start smaller. Is there a random, minor belief that can get us through the day…like Thoreau's "I believe I'll go canoeing"? Let's grab onto a belief that stirs us inside, even just a little, and let it carry us through the day.

Here's a belief that can help me make it through today:
I believe _____.

AUGUST 12

"Denial helps us to pace our feelings of grief. There is a grace in denial. It is nature's way of letting in only as much as we can handle."
— Elisabeth Kübler-Ross

Especially in the beginning of our grief, denial is our friend. It couldn't have happened. It didn't happen. There must be some mistake. It's just not possible. Denial helps us survive what would otherwise be unsurvivable.

Later on, denial is like a door we close when too much pain is rushing in. "That's enough reality for now!" we say, and we slam the door shut. Maybe tomorrow we can open the door again and let a little more hurt in.

Moderation in all things. Too much grief at once is bad, and so we dose ourselves with it. But too much denial is also bad, and so we must only allow ourselves doses of it.

I use denial to pace my grief. I shut the door, then open the door. Shut-open-shut-open.

AUGUST 13

"Grief is itself a medicine."
— William Cowper

You might hear grief described as an illness or a "condition" some time. That's because our scientific-method-obsessed, evidence-based discipline of medicine—which includes mental health—has tried to take ownership of grief and mourning.

But grief isn't an illness or disorder. It's the natural and necessary counterpart to having loved.

We don't need to be "treated" for our grief. There's nothing wrong with us. We just need to grieve and to express our grief. That's it. Nothing more; nothing less.

My grief is natural and necessary.
To feel and express my grief is to heal my grief.

AUGUST 14

"There was never a time when your life was not now,
nor will there ever be."
— Eckhart Tolle

While our grief naturally and necessarily takes us into our pasts
and leads us into our imagined futures, life, meanwhile,
is happening in the now.

Being present in the moment is a difficult way of being to
master, but it's worth working on. When you need a break from
your grief and mourning, try to focus on the here and now. Pay
attention to your breathing. In….. Out….. Notice the people,
objects, colors, and textures around you. Attend to the
sounds you hear. Smell the aromas in the air.
Really taste the food you are eating.

While we will always miss the person who died, focusing on the
present moment can provide breathing space.

When I need a break from my grief today,
I will focus on being present in the here and now.

AUGUST 15

"History is a set of lies agreed upon."
— Napoleon Bonaparte

Have you noticed there's a taboo against
speaking ill of the dead?

No one's perfect, including our loved ones who died. But after
death, we tend to downplay their shortcomings and focus
on—or even exaggerate—their best qualities. Hindsight may be
20/20—except when it comes to people who've died. Then it
tends to be more like 20/200, fuzzy and rose-colored.

Each of us has the right to remember those who died as we
choose. We each create our own stories, and in the process of
telling and retelling the stories, the sharp edges often get worn
smooth. Sometimes, though, we find ourselves revisiting painful
memories and bad feelings in our storytelling. That's OK, too.
It just means we need to explore and express them.

Anger, regret, shame, disgust—those feelings are as legitimate
as any other. If we share them outside of ourselves, even if it
means speaking ill of the dead, they will soften, allowing more
loving, compassionate feelings to come to the fore.

***I have the right to my own unique thoughts and feelings about
the person who died. My reality is my reality.***

AUGUST 16

"For the seed to achieve its greatest expression, it must come completely undone. The shell cracks, its insides come out, and everything changes. To someone who doesn't understand growth, it would look like complete destruction."

— Cynthia Occelli

People tell us we'll grow from this loss. They say we'll get wiser and stronger.

We don't want to grow! Give us back those who died, instead.

Eventually we'll see, though, that we are, in fact, changing. We've learned hard lessons. We're becoming different people— people who better understand what's really important, who appreciate others more, who are more likely to live out our passions and discard the rest.

Our shells are cracking and our insides are coming out. Like seeds that have been planted, we are experiencing not *annihilation* (which is what it feels like much of the time!) but instead *transformation*.

I am coming completely undone. I am transforming.

AUGUST 17

"I think I did pretty well, considering I started out with nothing but a bunch of blank paper."
— Steve Martin

Now there's a way to think about our lives. We start out with nothing but a bunch of blank paper—an empty canvas or a blank calendar. Then we start to live, and we slowly begin to fill in all that white space.

As we're living, we often feel like everything's a mess—like our paper is getting filled up with all kinds of mistakes and wasted opportunities and loss. But when we take a few steps away from the paper and look at it, we can see that our lives are beautiful and amazing. Besides, what's the alternative? The blank paper.

I think we're doing pretty well, considering we started out with nothing but a bunch of blank paper.

Everything's chaotic and mixed-up. I guess I'm doing pretty well.

AUGUST 18

"I don't like that man. I must get to know him better."
— Abraham Lincoln

When we don't like something or someone, our instinct is to distance ourselves from it. We look away. We move away.

We don't like our grief, so we try to ignore, suppress, or deny it. We look away whenever we can. We move away.

What we really need to do, though, is to get to know our grief better. We must move closer to it and befriend it. Because even though our instincts are telling us to run, we must remember that we are contaminated by our culture, which misunderstands the role of pain and suffering. As we learn to accept the necessity of grief, we will find the true and natural instinct to get to know our grief. It's been there deep inside us all along.

I don't like my grief. I must get to know it better.

AUGUST 19

"Smile, breathe, and go slowly."
— Thich Nhat Hanh

I think I will amend this quote to say: Smile or frown, breathe, and go slowly. In other words, we must feel and express whatever we are feeling, work on living in the moment, and be patient with ourselves.

That is perhaps the simplest recipe for healing in grief.

And aren't the simplest rules always the hardest to live by?

I will express my feelings, be present in the moment, and have patience with myself.

AUGUST 20

"Handle them carefully, for words can have more power than atom bombs."
— Pearl Strachan Hurd

People say ridiculous things to us when we're grieving. They usually don't mean to, but sometimes they hurt us with their words. "I know how you feel," they say. Or: "He's in a better place." Or: "You just need to be strong." Or: "Think of all you have to be thankful for." Or: "God wouldn't give you more than you can handle."

People offer clichés because they don't know what else to say. We ourselves have probably said such things to a grieving person at one time or another.

Yes, words are powerful. But the feelings behind them are even more powerful. When others speak to us in maddening platitudes, let's work on listening for the emotion behind the message. Usually it's: "I care about you and wish you didn't have to hurt like this."

I understand that most people don't know what to say to me. I will try to listen for the compassion behind the words.

AUGUST 21

"Trust yourself. You know more than you think you do."
— Benjamin Spock

Whom do we trust in life? We trust people who do what they say they will do. We trust people who act responsibly with other people, with belongings, and with information. We also trust experts—those who have the experience to know what they are talking about.

We are the experts of our own grief. We know more than we think we do. I've noticed that people often doubt their thoughts and feelings in grief; they tend to think they are "not normal" or even "bad." They do not trust in the just-rightness of their grief.

But our grief is exactly what it needs to be for us right now. If we acknowledge, embrace, and express our true thoughts and feelings, we are trusting in our grief. If we ignore, suppress, judge, or try to circumvent our true thoughts and feelings, we are not trusting in our grief. Trusting in ourselves leads to hope and healing; not trusting in ourselves leads to dying while we are alive.

I trust in my grief. It is leading me where I need to go.

AUGUST 22

"Let's always meet each other with a smile,
for a smile is the beginning of love."
— Mother Teresa

Some days we don't feel like smiling, and that's OK. But on the
days when smiling is possible, let's choose the simple act of
lifting the corners of our mouths as we make eye contact
with our fellow human beings.

A smile means, "I am glad to see you." It also means, "I am
your friend. I am kind. I am interested in you. I am open to
communicating with you." A smile, in other words,
is a powerful form of connection.

We need connection when we're grieving. We need to reach out
and invite others to reach back. A simple smile can be
the action that opens our hearts to others.

I'll smile and make eye contact as much as possible today.
My smile will open my life to empathy.

AUGUST 23

*"The sun shines and warms and lights us, and we have no curiosity to
know why this is so, but we ask the reason of all evil, of pain,
and hunger, and mosquitoes, and silly people."*

— Ralph Waldo Emerson

Why??? We have so many thoughts and questions about
why things turned out the way they did.

It's natural to ask why in the face of death and grief. But maybe
it's also helpful to ask why about what we think of as the good
things in our lives. Why is this flower so perfect? Why do I have
a friend who is so good to me? Why has the love in my life
been so wonderful and transformative?

Are there reasons for goodness?
Do love and joy have causes or a creator?

Sometimes, I think, the answers to our why questions about
the bad things can be found in our why questions
about the good things.

*Why is life sometimes so lovely, good, and meaningful?
That is my question for today.*

AUGUST 24

"Each small task of everyday life is part of the total harmony of the universe."

— Saint Thérèse of Lisiuex

We sure aren't getting much accomplished these days. Entire weeks—months, even—pass, and we still haven't mustered the energy to tackle any of the big tasks we've been telling ourselves we would.

Our grief saps our energy and steals our motivation. It soaks up all our attention. And that is at it should be. We must allow ourselves this time of fallow.

Let us acknowledge and celebrate the smallest tasks we accomplish in our everyday lives, for right now that may constitute our contribution to the total harmony of the universe.

Every small task I accomplish in my everyday life is a victory.

AUGUST 25

"Rain, after all, is only rain; it is not bad weather. So also, pain is only pain; unless we resist it, then it becomes torment."

— I Ching

We have been devastated by loss. We are tormented.

Yet what happens if we surrender to the pain instead of resisting it? It softens. It downgrades from a Category 1 to a Category 2 hurricane.

The central paradox of grief is that the very act of befriending our pain diminishes it. We hold the key to easing our own torment.

My pain is only pain, unless I resist it; then it becomes torment.

AUGUST 26

"If someone listens, or stretches out a hand, or whispers a kind word of encouragement, or attempts to understand a lonely person, extraordinary things begin to happen."
— Loretta Girzartis

Bearing witness to another's grief is a gift beyond measure. The smallest gesture can have a profound healing effect.

We exist in relation to other people. Our social connections give our lives meaning. Studies have shown that people who are in solitary confinement for long periods of time begin to hallucinate other people; their brains literally invent others to coexist and communicate with.

We can reach out to other people in small ways. And when other people reach out to us, we must learn to gratefully accept. It is at the points of connection that extraordinary things begin to happen.

When I connect with other caring human beings, extraordinary things begin to happen.

AUGUST 27

"My joy may be diminished now, but I am still alive
to be more joyful ahead."
— Ankam Nithin Kumar

Our joy is surely diminished now, but we are still alive. And
if we've learned anything about life, it's that it's constantly
changing, often in unpredictable ways.

Our lives are how they are right now. They're full of pain and
suffering. But they'll be different in the future. We can't predict
all the ways in which our lives will change, but we can count on
them being different. We can also set a course for more love
and joy ahead by claiming our intention to heal and by
actively exploring and expressing our grief.

As long as there is life, there is possibility.

My joy is diminished now, but I am still alive to experience
more joy, love, and meaning in the days ahead.

AUGUST 28

"I feel like a part of my soul has loved you since the beginning of everything. Maybe we're from the same star."

— Emery Allen

With one or sometimes a few special people in our lives, we share profoundly close bonds. We sometimes say we are soulmates with these people. Such relationships may be between lovers, friends, or family members.

When a soulmate dies, our grief is especially hard. We understood, opened fully to, served, and challenged each other. We were the heroes of each other's lives. But now that this person has died, we must learn to live without our champion and other half.

When a soulmate dies, we must mourn as we loved: heroically, grandly, and fully. Our grief will be as big as our love, and we must find equally grand ways in which to express it. This takes outsized courage and fortitude. We must be our own heroes on the quest for healing.

When my soulmate dies, the only way to heal my grieving soul is with mourning that is as large as my love.

AUGUST 29

"Intentions compressed into words enfold magical power."
— Deepak Chopra

Our words have the power to communicate to ourselves, to others, and to the universe what we think, what we feel, and what we intend to think, feel, and be in the future.

Language is magical. It's a tool both for self-understanding and for helping others understand.

Let's put our grief into words, either verbally or in writing. Let's put our intentions for healing our grief into words, too. Using words to capture and mold our inner truths gives them transformative power.

I will put my grief and my intentions for healing my grief into words.

AUGUST 30

"Self-worth comes from one thing—thinking that you are worthy."
— Dr. Wayne Dyer

Our grief can affect our self-esteem. If we blame ourselves for things having to do with the death, or if we shame ourselves for falling apart in grief, we can feel less-than. Not good enough. Miserably inadequate.

But we are worthy! It's just that the natural depression of our grief may be tricking us into believing that we are not. If clinical depression becomes part of our picture, our sense of self-worth may plummet even further.

You are worthy of healing and a continued life full of meaning, love, and joy. So am I. Each and every one of us is. We all deserve to achieve reconciliation in grief and go on to live and love well. If depression or other issues are eroding our sense of self-worth, in essence roadblocking our path to healing, we should seek the help of a professional caregiver. We deserve to heal, but we will not heal if we do not feel worthy of healing.

I am worthy of healing. I deserve a continued life full of meaning, love, and joy.

AUGUST 31

*"You can clutch the past so tightly to your chest that it leaves
your arms too full to embrace the present."*

— Jan Glidewell

Grief is always a balancing act. In the early days and weeks, we
are so overwhelmed by our loss that we can do little else—and
yet we still have to eat and bathe and sleep. At some point we
have to go to work, take care of children, go grocery shopping,
pay our bills—whatever our daily lives require of us.

In other words, we must grieve and mourn *while we are living*.
They become part of the activities of our lives. And how much
time and energy we devote to them versus all our other life
responsibilities is the balancing act we try to figure out
anew every day. We don't always get it right.

Sometimes we focus so much on our loss that we forsake our
present lives. This is normal and even necessary at first, but
eventually we must find a good balance. The more actively we
mourn, the more the teeter-totter will begin to tip toward
our new lives without the person who died.

I'm working on balancing mourning and living.
need to do both.

SEPTEMBER 1

"Optimism is a strategy for making a better future. Because unless you believe that the future can be better, you are unlikely to step up and take responsibility for making it so."

— Noam Chomsky

It can be hard to be optimistic in grief. Through no fault of our own, loss has torn us apart. Life is painful and terrible. Why go on living when there's surely just more pain to come?

Yet we hold onto hope, which is an expectation of a good that is yet to be. We will take the bargain that even though there is also more bad yet to be, the good will outweigh the bad.

We are responsible for ourselves in this journey called grief. We are responsible for taking good care of ourselves, for mourning actively and openly, for being gentle and self-compassionate. First we foster hope, then we nurture optimism, then we step up and take responsibility for doing what needs to be done, one day at a time. That is our strategy.

I believe that the future will be better.
I will step up and take responsibility for making it so.

SEPTEMBER 2

"A man's dying is more the survivor's affair than his own."
— Thomas Mann

Sometimes our loved ones tell us what they would like to happen (or not to happen) after they die. Do this with my body, they say. Do or don't have a funeral/move/remarry/take care of ourselves/etc.

Honoring their wishes is necessary, right? Hm. Not always. What if your needs or your family's needs conflict with those wishes?

I often emphasize, for example, that funerals are for the living. When someone says, "Don't have a funeral for me...," we need to remember that the funeral really isn't for him. It's for us. The transformative power of ritual can help us in so many ways at a time when nothing else will.

We're the ones who need to go on living until we, too, die. I believe that sometimes we have to trust that the person who died is now enlightened about the possible folly of some of the orders he left behind—and he now has grace about our decisions to do what is best for us who remain here on earth.

I will do what is best for me and the other survivors, and I will trust that the person who died is cheering us on.

SEPTEMBER 3

*"Presence cannot be easily defined. Presence can only be experienced.
But I know this: True presence to someone or something allows
them or it to change me and influence me—
before I try to change them or it!"*

— Richard Rohr

Grief cannot be easily defined. Grief can only be experienced.

When we are present to our grief, we are paying attention to it.
We are opening ourselves to it. We are embracing it—whatever
it looks and feels like in that particular moment.

When we are present to our grief, we are allowing ourselves to
be changed by it. We are not trying to change our grief;
instead, we are accepting it as it is.

It takes courage, practice, and time to be truly present to our
grief. It also takes courage, practice, and time to express—
or mourn—our grief. We are working on both.

I am working on being present to and expressing my grief.

SEPTEMBER 4

"Ah," I smiled. "I'm not really here to keep you from freaking out. I'm here to be with you while you freak out, or grieve or laugh or suffer or sing. It is a ministry of presence. It is showing up with a loving heart."
— Kate Braestrup

We need people who can be present to us in our grief. Who can be here with us while we cry or talk or scream or sit in silence. Who don't think it's their job to keep us from freaking out. Who bear witness without being overbearing. Who accompany without taking over or slipping away.

I've noticed that about one-third of the people in our lives are capable of showing up with a loving heart and a ministry of presence. Another third can't really help in this way but don't hurt us either. And the final third are often toxic and harmful to our healing. They may tell us to quit mourning or declare that we're doing it wrong.

This "rule of thirds" is good to keep in mind. We should steer clear of that last third, and when we're fortunate to meet someone in the first third, someone who's blessed with a ministry of presence, we'll know whom to turn to when we need companionship on our journey.

I need people who show up with a loving heart.
When I am gifted with their ministry of presence,
I will muster the courage to actively mourn.

SEPTEMBER 5

"It's called grief work because finding your way through grief is hard work. If you put it off like a messy chore, it just sits there waiting for you."

— Marty Tousley

Around Labor Day I sometimes think about how much we labor in grief. Grief and mourning are hard work! In fact, they might be the hardest work we've ever done in our entire lives.

Our grief and mourning are exhausting. If we give them the time and attention and effort they demand, they wear us out. Our grief labors deplete us physically, cognitively, emotionally, socially, and spiritually.

So maybe Labor Day is a day to take respite from our grief work. We can choose to treat it as a holiday from our grief. We have been working hard, and we need a day of rest. If we don't give ourselves some much-needed downtime, we might burn out. Let's spend this day doing whatever recharges us.

My grief and mourning labors are exhausting.
I will take a day off when I need one.

SEPTEMBER 6

*"Trust that your soul has a plan, and even if you can't see it all,
know that everything will unfold as it is meant to."*
— Deepak Chopra

Our souls have been injured by loss.
Can injured souls have a plan?

Yes, I believe our injured souls will guide us to hope and
healing—if we only let them take the lead. They instinctively
know what they need to reconcile our grief. They need to shed
tears. They need to talk about their injuries. They need the
balm of love and friendship.

It is the ego that often smothers the soul's wisdom. Brainwashed
by our mourning-avoidant culture, our egos try to boss our
souls around. "Quit crying," our egos say. "You're strong. You
can handle this. The rest of the people in your life need you
to pick up the pieces and carry on."

If we still ourselves and allow our deepest, truest voice to be
heard above the ego's tyranny, it will tell us what to do.
Our souls have a plan.

My soul has a plan. I will listen to my soul.

SEPTEMBER 7

"Sadness flies away on the wings of time."
— Jean de La Fontaine

This is probably the biggest misconception there is about grief. "Time heals all wounds," people say. "Just hang on. The more time that passes, the better you'll feel."

I sometimes wish that time alone would heal my grief. But it doesn't. Yes, the passage of months and years does tend to blunt and blur our feelings, but unless we're also actively mourning our grief as time passes, those feelings will only grow more complicated. They'll come out in other ways, like chronic depression, anxiety, or addiction.

We need to feel it to heal it. And we need to express it. If we buy into the misconception that time alone will work that magic, we're setting ourselves up for a lifetime of merely existing instead of really living.

I know that time alone cannot heal my wounds.
Only active mourning can do that.

SEPTEMBER 8

"The death of a beloved is an amputation."
— C.S. Lewis

We grievers are torn apart. When the special people we love died, a part of us was cut off. We survive as amputees of a sort.

Amputees who lose a physical limb often experience phantom pain. Their missing limbs physically hurt them—even though they're not there. Our missing people hurt us—even though they're not here. We hurt physically, cognitively, emotionally, socially, and spiritually.

There is no getting back the parts of ourselves we lost. There is only learning to manage without them. The process of grief and mourning is our rehabilitation. The more we actively work at it, the more capably and fully we will be able to live the rest of our days.

I have experienced an amputation,
and I am committed to my rehabilitation.

SEPTEMBER 9

"Sorrow and scarlet leaf,
Sad thoughts and sunny weather.
Ah me, this glory and this grief
Agree not well together!"

— Thomas Parsons, *A Song for September*

Some days are too beautiful for grief. It's as if nature disrespects
the darkness we are feeling inside. It can doubly anger us when
we realize that the person who died would have loved
the opportunity to experience this gorgeous day.

So what do we do when we have such a mismatch inside and
out? I find that when this happens, if I coax myself outdoors
and spend some time being present to nature's glory, I usually
achieve a bit of movement in my grief. I might have a good cry
as I walk through the woods. I might rake leaves, giving my
body something repetitive to do as my heart and soul ask their
"why?" questions. Or I might have a silent conversation with
the person who died, telling her how unfair it is that
she can't enjoy this day with me.

Dissonance and tension are often springboards
to forward movement.

Sad thoughts and sunny weather can
work together to help me heal.

SEPTEMBER 10

"A feeling of pleasure or solace can be so hard to find when you are in the depths of your grief. Sometimes it's the little things that help get you through the day. You may think your comforts sound ridiculous to others, but there is nothing ridiculous about finding one little thing to help you feel good in the midst of pain and sorrow!"

— Elizabeth Berrien

It seems silly how little things can help us cope sometimes. For me, when I'm deeply grieving, something as simple as a breathing in and out or as ridiculous as a silly movie (*What About Bob?* is a personal favorite) can make me feel like I can go on another hour or two.

In grief, the little things are the big things. We need our little moments of pleasure or solace. It's like we're climbing a treacherous mountain and those trinkets are our handholds. We're not just happy to have them; some days it feels like they're literally saving our lives!

When we're struggling, we can make a list of the little things that give us pleasure or comfort. If we carry the list in our phones, purses, or wallets, we'll always have a reminder about where to find the next handhold.

Three little things that give me pleasure or solace—that's how many I'm going to go out of my way to grab hold of today.

SEPTEMBER 11

"One and one are sometimes eleven."
— Kashmiri Proverb

I've often observed that when we're in grief, having just one other person who will spend time with us, listen to us when we want to talk, and generally keep us company can be enough.

We don't necessarily need a whole team of helpers who can be present to our grief (although we should feel fortunate if we do). No, just one single fellow human being who is a good, nonjudgmental listener and is readily available when we need him can sometimes be the difference between hell and healing.

Sometimes one plus one equals a whole lot more than two.

If I have one good helper, I will thank her today.
If I don't yet have at least one good helper,
I will reach out to someone new today.

SEPEMBER 12

"Sanctuary, on a personal level, is where we perform the job of taking care of our soul."
— Christopher Forrest McDowell

When grief, loss, and the need to mourn enter our lives, we need a dedicated, safe space to call our own. We need a private territory where we can explore self-development and spiritual practices as well as read insightful books, meditate, journal, or simply contemplate the universe.

Each of us can choose our own personal grief sanctuary. It may be "your" seat or pew in your place of worship. It could be a garden in a park or a hiking path, or a bench on the grounds of a retreat center. Sanctuaries are usually sanctified in some way to invite in and help us connect to the Divine. We can create a sacred space in our home by smudging the room or adorning it with items or furniture that help our minds focus on our spiritual selves. We can say a special prayer or chant to designate that it is set apart from other rooms in our home as a sacred space.

Our sanctuaries are where we go to grieve when our souls need time for inward focus. Our sanctuaries are calm, safe, and comforting.

I will designate a sanctuary for my grief.

SEPTEMBER 13

"A child can live with anything as long as he or she is told the truth and is allowed to share with loved ones the natural feelings people have when they are suffering."

— Eda LeShan

If we have grieving children in our lives, we have the opportunity to help them. You see, many grown-ups mistakenly believe that it is kinder to hide loss, grief, and mourning from children than it is to expose them to the pain of life…but the truth is, we can't hide loss, grief, and mourning from them.

Any child old enough to love is old enough to mourn. When someone we love dies, we grieve. When someone a child loves dies, the child grieves. And even when we are grieving the loss of someone the child is not attached to, the child reads our grief in our every gesture.

Children can handle the truth. What they can't handle are half-truths, omissions, or outright lies. We can help them by sharing the truth at their developmental level of understanding and modeling open mourning.

I will help the grieving children in my life.
If I am too overwhelmed by my own grief to help them,
I will appoint another kind, responsible adult to help.

SEPTEMBER 14

"A moment comes when the true self reveals itself. That moment comes when you are willing to be unconditionally present in the imperfection of this moment. A simple change of attitude; instead of chasing after perfection, you allow a total and profound surrendering to the imperfection of the moment."

— Tyohar

When you think about it, every moment is imperfect in grief because in every moment, the people we love are not here. It is this very absence that ruins every moment. And even if these people would not have been physically here beside us in this moment anyway, our knowing that they are also not elsewhere on earth, living their lives, renders this moment imperfect.

All we can do is learn to live in the imperfection of this moment, which may include many good things. The comfort of our chair. The light through the trees. The company of someone we care about.

In surrendering to the imperfection of this moment, we relinquish the very idea of perfection. And once we let that go, we can appreciate all that *is* good, now.

Today is imperfect. Tomorrow will be imperfect too. I can choose to cultivate gratitude for the good-but-not-perfect.

SEPTEMBER 15

"People in mourning have to come to grips with death before they can live again. Mourning can go on for years and years. It doesn't end after a year; that's a false fantasy. It usually ends when people realize that they can live again, and they can concentrate their energies on their lives as a whole, and not on their hurt, and guilt, and pain."

— Elisabeth Kübler-Ross

We must come to grips with the death before we can truly live again. While I don't agree with Dr. Kübler-Ross that grief ever discretely "ends" (it softens and erupts less frequently as, over time, we do the work of mourning), I do agree that through embracing the hurt and pain we can emerge into a place of renewed wholeness.

For now we appropriately focus our energies on our grief. We do this because grief is our truth. Over time, the focusing of energy on and expressing of our grief transports us. Ever so slowly, we begin to transcend the pain. Then, the passions and loves of our changed lives become our new truth.

We concentrate our energies on our grief so that we can integrate it into our beings. One day we will again be able to concentrate our energies on our lives as a whole.

I trust that I will learn to live again. For now, I will concentrate my energies on my grief and mourning.

SEPTEMBER 16

"There is a land of the living and a land of the dead, and the bridge is love, the only survival, the only meaning."

— Thornton Wilder

We live in this world. Our special people who have died live in that other world. We are separated from them, and the separation is painful beyond measure.

But there's a bridge from our world to theirs. It's called love. We still love them, and our undying love connects us to them. And their love for us? It is also everlasting, and if we work to tune into it, we can still feel it flowing from that world back to us.

I'm so grateful for the bridge.

Love is the only survival. It is the only meaning. I choose love.

SEPTEMBER 17

"Sometimes your only available transportation is a leap of faith."
— Margaret Shepard

Now and then in grief we reach a chasm. It's like the yawning Grand Canyon stands between us and the path we know leads to healing. If we stay where we are, we'll be stuck forever. But it seems impossible to move forward, too. What are we supposed to do?

We're supposed to leap. We're supposed to take by the hand the scariest, wildest idea we have about regaining momentum in our grief—and jump.

It takes a leap of faith sometimes to get unstuck, hurdle an impasse, or get to the other side of what seems like an uncrossable canyon.

One, two, three…jump!

Sometimes my only available transportation
might be a leap of faith.

SEPTEMBER 18

"When the rhythms of our body-mind are in sync with nature's rhythms, when we are living in harmony with life, we are living in the state of grace. To live in grace is to experience that state of consciousness where things flow effortlessly and our desires are easily fulfilled. Grace is magical, synchronistic, coincidental, joyful. It's that good-luck factor. But to live in grace we have to allow nature's intelligence to flow through us without interfering."

— Deepak Chopra

Our grief is part of nature's intelligence. We are born knowing how to love and also how to grieve. We mourn instinctually, although our contemporary Western culture's denial of death and pain can make us doubt the naturalness of our grief and mourning.

When we embrace our grief and mourn openly and naturally, we are opening ourselves to grace. Instead of fighting with and hampering ourselves, we welcome ourselves. We live in tender honesty. And grace comes flowing in.

I trust in the naturalness of grief and mourning. The more I embrace and express my grief, the more I open myself to grace.

SEPTEMBER 19

"Lord, have mercy, because I am in misery. My eyes are weak from so much crying, and my whole being is tired from grief."

— Psalm 31:9

Mercy is compassion shown toward someone you have the power to harm. In other words, mercy is when people who could hurt us treat us with kindness instead.

We are tired and hurting. We need mercy, not only from God but from our fellow human beings. We need our bosses to lighten our workloads and allow us time to grieve and mourn. We need our neighbors to smile and lend a helping hand. We need our friends not to judge and to be patient. We need our family members to allow us to grieve and mourn in our own unique ways.

We need mercy.

Here is the message—silent or spoken—I will send out to others today: Have mercy, because I am in misery.

SEPTEMBER 20

"My desire to live is as intense as ever, and though my heart is broken, hearts are made to be broken: that is why God sends sorrow into the world... To me, suffering seems now a sacramental thing that makes whose whom it touches holy."

— Oscar Wilde

If we believe in God or a higher power, we may well be asking ourselves "Why?" Why did God allow this person to die? Why now? Why in this way? Asking such "Why?" questions is normal and necessary in grief.

Does God send sorrow into the world for a reason? Many of the great philosophers and spiritual thinkers have weighed in on this question. In the quote for today, Oscar Wilde says that hearts are made to be broken. I guess I would have to agree, because I believe that hearts are made to love, and being broken is the unavoidable corollary.

If love is holy, then grief, too, is holy. Both are sacramental, transformative experiences.

My heart loved, so now it is broken.
My love and my grief are the very essence of life.

SEPTEMBER 21

"To be interested in the changing seasons is a happier state of mind than to be hopelessly in love with spring."

— George Santayana

Fall is upon us. Once again, the seasons are changing. Time marches ever forward.

I love fall, so I generally look forward to September. But today Mr. Santayana has me considering that maybe I should work on cultivating an appreciation for the ever-changing nature of life.

Death is change. For those left behind, it's a hard change—but it's also inevitable and, sometimes, expected. Grieving is our process of learning to live with the change, to embrace our new normal.

We were hopelessly in love with the people who died. Yet like spring, they came…then they left. Can we learn to be interested in what we are experiencing now? We are trying.

I am working on being interested in the now of life.
I am working on embracing change.

SEPTEMBER 22

"Art enables us to find ourselves and lose ourselves at the same time."
— Thomas Merton

Making art when we're in grief can be a powerful way to mourn. When we sketch, paint, take photos, assemble a collage, write a poem or song, craft, make a mini-movie, or participate in any kind of artistic endeavor, we can channel our thoughts and feelings about our loss into our art.

If you like to be creative, try making something that expresses what's inside you. If you don't normally like creating art or believe you're not good at it, give it a go anyway. Pair up with someone you know who has the materials and interest and ask her to help you get started.

Of course, viewing art can also be cathartic. Consider reading a book, visiting an art gallery, or seeing a film with themes of love and loss.

Whether we make or appreciate art, we may at once lose ourselves in the experience and find a new bit of understanding or peace.

To engage with my grief, I will make or appreciate a piece of art today.

SEPTEMBER 23

"Keep on going, and the chances are that you will stumble on something, perhaps when you are least expecting it. I never heard of anyone ever stumbling on something sitting down."
— Charles F. Kettering

Grief is passive and internal. Mourning is active and external. We grieve first, then we put our grief into action through mourning.

It's when we're actively mourning that we stumble onto things. We stumble onto compassion when someone sees we're mourning and reaches out to help us. We stumble onto gratitude when we encounter small, unexpected blessings. We stumble onto hope when we are exposed to new opportunities.

Sometimes we do need to sit down with our grief, silent and alone. But when we put it into motion, over and over we find ourselves stumbling onto grace.

C'mon, grief. It's time to get moving.

SEPTEMBER 24

"Never be afraid to fall apart, because it is an opportunity to rebuild yourself the way you wish you had been all along."

— Rae Smith

Our grief has shattered us into a million pieces. We've fallen apart, all right.

One thing's for sure: We can't put the pieces back together just as they were. We're different now. We've changed.

Maybe we can start from our shatteredness and build something new from the shards. Maybe this is an opportunity to be who we might have been.

Of course, we'd trade our new, improving selves for having our special people back for one minute if we could…but we can't. I figure we owe it to our loved ones who died to rebuild ourselves the way we wish we had been all along.

My grief has shattered me into a million pieces.
Now I have the opportunity to rebuild myself the way
I wish I had been all along.

SEPTEMBER 25

"A yes to feelings is a station stop before we get to philosophical explanations, theological consolations, or encouraging maxims."
— David Richo

It is tempting to push aside our painful feelings in grief. We yearn for something—anything—that will ease our pain. A simple answer, that's what we're looking for.

But philosophical explanations, theological consolations, and encouraging maxims aren't quick fixes. They are all things we will consider and maybe even find comfort in during our journey, but they are no substitute for feeling what we feel.

Along the way, we must say yes to whatever we feel. If we're feeling angry, we must acknowledge, embrace, and express our anger. If we're feeling sad or afraid or guilty, ditto. For some of us, saying yes to our feelings takes practice. But it is an essential station stop on the journey to healing.

Today and every day, I will say yes to my feelings.

SEPTEMBER 26

"Our grief, though naturally difficult, is a source of energy within us. When we outwardly mourn, we unleash this amazing healing force."
— Alan Wolfelt

Our grief often drains us of energy and makes us feel lethargic and listless. So how can our grief be a source of energy within us?

We've been emphasizing that the outward expression of grief is called mourning. It is mourning that gives motion to our grief.

We can think of our grief like gasoline. Stored up inside us, it is inert. But when we ignite it and run it through the engine of life, we are burning it, as author Kenji Miyazawa famously said, as fuel for our journey.

Activated grief is an amazing healing force. Each day we will burn a bit more of our grief as fuel for our journey.

My grief is stored energy. I will burn some through active mourning today and notice the momentum this creates.

SEPTEMBER 27

"It is better to light one small candle than to curse the darkness."
— Confucius

Because we were raised in a time and culture that eschews grief
and darkness, we often curse them. We hate death.
We hate loss. We hate grief.

Yet darkness is as central to the human experience as is light.
Why curse something that is essential and unavoidable?

Paradoxically, if we instead learn to embrace the "dark"
experiences of life, we are lighting a candle of hope. We are
saying, "Darkness, we honor you. We are ready to pay
attention to you and get to know you."

This thinking and being changes everything. It banishes
fear and fosters hope.

*I am learning to stop cursing the darkness and instead
embrace it. This lights my candle of hope.*

SEPTEMBER 28

"Just when I discovered the meaning of life, they changed it."
— George Carlin

Boy do we know this feeling. We thought we'd figured out some things about life when all of a sudden—*wham*! Now everything is topsy-turvy, what was up is down, and we're desperately trying to make sense of it all again.

It's natural for the death of someone we love to raise all kinds of meaning-of-life-and-death questions. It's also natural for us to search for answers. We want answers because we want to feel settled again.

The thing is, it usually takes a long time and a lot of figuring out for us to arrive at a new understanding of the meaning of life. For now, all we can do is keep questioning and searching. There is meaning in that, too.

I'll try to be patient—with myself in particular and with life in general—as I do the long, hard work of rediscovering the meaning of life.

SEPTEMBER 29

"I think prime numbers are like life. They are very logical, but you could never work out the rules, even if you spend all your time thinking about them."

— Mark Haddon

So, 29 is a prime number (which means a number evenly divisible only by itself and 1). I'm not really a math guy, but I do understand that much.

Mathematicians are always trying to figure out problems and equations with irreducible logic. That is their discipline. But prime numbers pose mathematical riddles that the world's brightest math geniuses have still not been able to solve.

I have learned that grief is similarly immune to logic. Oh sure, we can talk about it at length and try to capture it with words and stories. But like love, grief is, at bottom, a spiritual experience beyond the capabilities of language.

We can talk and think all we want about the equations of grief, but what really matters is our unique, particular, and unquantifiable experience.

I can't work out the rules to grief. I can only experience it, embrace it, and do my best to express it every day.

SEPTEMBER 30

"Thirty days hath September…"
— Mother Goose

Each day can feel over-long in grief. When we're in pain and finding no pleasure or meaning in our daily routines, every 24-hour rotation of the earth can seem like a lifetime.

And September? September may only have 30 days— an average month—but it's gone on and on and on.

Maybe it helps to understand that this slowing down of time is a normal and natural part of grief. It forces us to encounter our thoughts and feelings. It makes our grief inescapable, which can be seen as a good and necessary thing. We *need* to encounter it.

If we feel too restless or in despair during our slow-mo grief days, we can use the time to actively express our grief. Typically hours fly by when we are pouring out our hearts and souls to a good listener. We can also move our bodies. Long walks, swims, or bike rides not only literally transport us, the endorphins they release also transport our hearts and souls, giving us respite from our relentless pain.

The slow-mo of my grief serves a purpose. I can surrender to it, or I can use the "extra" time to actively mourn.

OCTOBER 1

"I myself have often longed for some structure and theory that would compartmentalize or chart my pain. But, there is no single story or timetable or passageway through sorrow."
— Helen Vozenilek

We've heard of the "stages" of grief, popularized in 1969 by Elisabeth Kübler-Ross's landmark text, *On Death and Dying*. In this book she lists the five stages of grief that she saw terminally ill patients experience in the face of their own impending deaths: denial, anger, bargaining, depression, and acceptance. However, she never intended for her five stages to be applied to all grief or to be interpreted as a rigid, linear sequence to be followed by all mourners.

The truth is, there is no set structure or single route through grief. There are needs we must all meet—acknowledging the reality of the death; embracing the pain; remembering the person who died; developing a new self-identity; searching for meaning; and accepting help from others—but there is no certain order or timetable in which we must do it.

We think what we think. We feel what we feel.
It takes as long as it takes.

I have the right to my unique grief and mourning.
On this journey, only I can be the guide. I will meet my
mourning needs in ways that work for me, and I will
try to be patient and gentle with myself.

OCTOBER 2

"I'm so glad I live in a world where there are Octobers."
— L.M. Montgomery

Fall is my favorite season, but sometimes I'm so caught up in my grief or in the busy-ness of my life that I neglect to slow down and appreciate the kaleidoscope of leaves and the crispness in the air.

It's a good reminder for us grievers. Even when we're doing the necessary work of going deep inside ourselves and embracing our grief, we can find renewal and refreshment in regular appreciation breaks—no matter the season.

If I consciously choose to stop what I'm doing or thinking about and pay attention to the now of my existence, if only for five minutes, I'm sure to notice something to be glad about.

I'm so glad I live in a world where there are so many marvelous experiences.

OCTOBER 3

"'I could have.' What does this phrase mean? At any given moment in our lives, there are certain things that could have happened, but didn't. The magic moments go unrecognized, and then suddenly, the hand of destiny changes everything."
— Paulo Coelho

If only. We have so many "if onlys" now. If only she hadn't… If only I would have… If only there had been… Our regrets and unfulfilled wishes may torment us. It's normal to think about what could have been. With the benefit of hindsight, our minds and hearts can't help but see how things could have been otherwise.

When we talk through our feelings of regret aloud, in the company of a caring listener, we come to understand the limits of our own culpability. Rarely are we actually at fault. Neither we nor the person who died nor others involved are perfect. As Maya Angelou said, "I did then what I knew how to do. Now that I know better, I do better."

What's more, in telling the story of our regrets we grow to understand that much of what happens in life is beyond our control. Our "if onlys" represent our wish to control. When we surrender to the truth that no human can control life, our "if onlys" begin to lose their power.

I have "if onlys." Whenever they're weighing on my heart and mind, I'll speak them aloud to someone who can listen without dismissing them.

OCTOBER 4

"After (her) death I began to see her as she had really been.
It was less like losing someone than discovering someone."
— Nancy Halle

After those we love die, we are forced to shift our relationship
with them from one of presence to one of memory. We slowly
grow to understand that our memories, though often
painful at first, are our treasures.

But remembering our own personal experiences with those
who have died is not the only way our understanding of them
is shaped. After a death, other people share *their* memories and
assessments with us. We are often hungry for more stories. We
learn things we didn't know. We come to new realizations.
Our portraits of those who died may shift and change.

In this way, we rediscover our loved ones who have died.
Sometimes we like our changed perceptions, and sometimes we
do not. Either way, the dead often change as we change, which
only goes to show that even death is powerless against
the universe's constant motion.

As I am rediscovering myself, I am also rediscovering you.

OCTOBER 5

*"All sorrows can be borne if you put them in a story
or tell a story about them."*

—Isak Dinesen

Love is never the same twice, and neither is grief. Each is a one-of-a-kind story, a snowflake in the history of humanity. Part of our grief work now is to tell our stories. We find comfort and support when we surround ourselves with people who will honor our stories of love and loss.

Because stories of love and loss take time, patience, and unconditional love, they serve as powerful antidotes to a modern society that is all too often preoccupied with getting us to "let go," "move on," and "get closure." Whether we share our stories with a friend, a family member, a coworker, or a fellow traveler in grief, having others bear witness to the telling of our unique stories is one way to go backward on the pathway to eventually going forward.

We heal ourselves as we tell the tale. This is the awesome power of story.

I will find ways to tell my story of love and loss.

OCTOBER 6

"Normal is a relative term; I have yet to meet this 'normal' person."
— Ken Poirot

Because I travel the world speaking about grief and mourning, and because I've written many books on the subject, mourners approach me every day with their questions. One of the most common questions I get is some variation on this:

I've been experiencing_____. Is that normal?

The answer is always yes. Whatever you're thinking, feeling, or experiencing is what's normal for you given your circumstances.

Sometimes losses are abnormally traumatic, however. In these cases, your grief may be more complicated, but it is still a normal response to an abnormally severe psychic injury. If this applies to you, I urge you to get extra support. An experienced grief counselor can offer you the equivalent of an ICU for your traumatic grief.

My grief is normal. I am normal.
There is nothing wrong with me or my grief.

OCTOBER 7

"Rain usually makes me feel mellow. Curl up in the corner time, slow down, smell the furniture. Today it just makes me feel wet."

— Jeff Melvoin

I bet you could fill in these blanks with lots of "usuallys": _____ usually makes me feel _____. But now that I'm grieving, it makes me feel _____.

Our grief has a way of affecting our every experience. We can't count on things we used to enjoy being enjoyable now. And some things that were neutral to us before are now minefields of tender emotion.

Have you heard the phrase "casting a pall over everything"? The word "pall" literally means a cloth spread over a coffin, hearse, or tomb—or a dark cloud or covering of smoke or dust. Our grief can cast a pall over everything. It can make most anything we encounter seem painful, gloomy, or just blah.

We're mired in the pall. But if we keep mourning, the pall, thank goodness, will begin to lift.

My grief is casting a pall over everything. For now, this is normal and necessary.

OCTOBER 8

"The angels are always near to those who are grieving, to whisper to
them that their loved ones are safe in the hand of God."

— Eileen Elias Freeman

The archangel Azriel is a figure in various religions and cultures.
Essentially, he is portrayed as an angel who accompanies
people who have died to heaven then returns to earth
to comfort those left behind.

I am open to the mystery of angels. How lovely it is to think
that our loved ones, as they lay dying, were taken by the hand
and shepherded to heaven. And how comforting it is to think
that we can turn to an unseen but present angel
whenever we need help in our grief.

Believing in angels is a form of trusting that all will be well. As
our intermediaries, angels connect the here with the hereafter.
They embody our faith. They are couriers of hope.
What's not to like?

Whether or not I believe in angels, I can choose to believe
that all will be well.

OCTOBER 9

"Tonight all the hells of young grief have opened up again; the mad words, the bitter resentment, the fluttering in the stomach, the nightmare reality, the wallowed-in tears. For in grief nothing 'stays put.' One keeps on emerging from a phase, but it always recurs. Round and round. Everything repeats."

— C.S. Lewis

If young or new love is exquisite, then young grief is torturous. They balance each other on the seesaw of human experience. Heaven and hell.

But even after we have survived and emerged from the very early days and weeks of our grief, we sometimes find ourselves revisiting young grief's intensely painful thoughts and feelings. The hurt and frustration can fill us with despair.

Healing in grief is a slow and spiraling process. We must trust that active mourning will, over time, soften even our most intense grief. Only with distant hindsight might we be able to see that each time we spiraled back on a certain thought or feeling, it was actually getting a tiny bit easier— though it may not have seemed so at the time.

In grief, everything repeats…but more softly, like a strident drumbeat that ever-so-slowly quiets and fades into the background.

OCTOBER 10

"I've had the kind of day no quote can fix."
— Richelle E. Goodrich

This book attempts to provide a daily smidgen of compassion
and hope to grievers. Because of its one-day-at-a-time format,
I offer a new thought or idea each day—but something
concise, so it's not overwhelming.

Some days, though, this concise profoundness, in the form of
quotes and meditations, can seem overly glib. Our grief can't be
gathered, corralled, and tamed like that. It's much too big and
overwhelming to be mollified by a few clever words
of empathy and advice.

If you ever pick up this book to read the day's thoughts and find
them puny in the face of what you're experiencing, know that
I understand. Set the book aside and share your thoughts
and feelings with a good listener instead.

The answer to my grief doesn't fit on a refrigerator magnet.
I can ignore "words of wisdom" whenever I feel like it.

OCTOBER 11

"There are genuine mysteries in the world that mark the limits of human knowing and thinking. Wisdom is fortified, not destroyed, by understanding its limitations."

— Mortimer J. Adler

I love to learn. In my work with grieving people and grief caregivers, as well as in my other passions, I am always eager to learn and grow in my understanding. I never think of myself as an expert but instead a devoted student.

And yet I also know that I can't know everything. Not only is there not enough time for me to learn everything, not everything is knowable by human beings. One only has to watch the videos online that depict Earth's place in the solar system, then the galaxy, then the universe to realize that there is so very much beyond our current understanding and mastery.

To me, human life and death are still mysteries…not so much the "hows" as the "whys." We as a species can only ever be wise to a point. What might lie beyond is a thrilling exercise in imagination and faith. Acknowledging our cognitive limitations opens us up to a whole universe of possibilities.

When I cannot under-stand, I can embrace "standing under" the mystery.

OCTOBER 12

"Those who have gone 'down' are the only ones who understand 'up.'"
— Richard Rohr

We understand down. Some days and weeks we inhabit down. And there is no deeper down than the grief that follows the death of someone precious to us.

While down is painful, it is also normal and necessary sometimes. Yet from the depths of our down, we can still look up. We can remember times of love and joy. We can connect with others we love and who love us back. And we can schedule moments of levity, entertainment, and distraction into our down days, such as watching a movie or playing with a pet.

We understand up. We can invite some up into our down. And we can also hold onto hope for more up in our futures.

I understand 'down,' but that is because I also understand 'up.'
I will give myself 'up' breaks in the middle of my downs.

OCTOBER 13

"Never forget that God is your friend. And like all friends, He longs to hear what's been happening in your life. Good or bad, whether it's been full of sorrow or anger, and even when you're questioning why terrible things have to happen."

— Nicholas Sparks

Sometimes we mistakenly believe that our grief dishonors our faith. After all, if we have faith, we shouldn't be sad about death. In fact, we should rejoice! Our religious training or affiliation may only reinforce this misconception.

But God made us to love, which means He also made us to grieve. And if He is our friend, He will compassionately bear witness to all of our human thoughts and feelings. Having a relationship with God means we can take everything to Him, including questioning our faith.

So let's be clear on this point: Having faith and grieving are not mutually exclusive. Even if we believe that one day we are to be reunited with our loved ones who have died, we still miss their presence here on earth.

I can have faith and grieve. I can also question my faith. God understands and accepts all of me.

OCTOBER 14

"Grief can't be shared. Everyone carries it alone,
his own burden, his own way."
— Anne Morrow Lindbergh

Misconception alert! Grief *can* be shared. Sharing our grief
outside of ourselves is called mourning, and
mourning is how we heal.

Ms. Lindbergh's statement is a common misconception, though,
so it's one we need to be on guard for. It's easy to swallow it hook,
line, and sinker. And when we do, we're setting ourselves up for
stuffing our grief down deep inside and never reconciling it.

Yes, we each grieve uniquely, and each of us has to find the self-
motivation and courage to actively mourn. Those parts are true.
But we are not alone in our grief. The more often we
act on that truth, the better.

My grief is uniquely my own, but I also
need others to help me with it.

OCTOBER 15

"Think what a better world it would be if we all, the whole world, had cookies and milk about three o'clock every afternoon and then lay down on our blankets for a nap."

— Barbara Jordan

Do you ever find yourself wanting your blankie? Lots of us have—or had, when we were little—a security object—something that soothed us whenever we held onto it. Maybe it's time for a security object for our journey through grief.

Here are some ideas: flannel pajamas; a cozy robe; down slippers; a plush blanket; a stuffed animal; a special pillow; a soft sweater. The object might be new, used, or even something that belonged to the person who died. Whenever we're deeply feeling our grief, we can grab hold of our security object and give ourselves some time to cry or just breathe.

We're never too old for cookies and milk, naps, and blankies.

I feel soothed when I hold onto_____.
I need and deserve soothing.

OCTOBER 16

"For fast-acting relief, try slowing down."
— Lily Tomlin

When we're in grief, we often want to get through it as quickly
as possible. After all, it hurts. It's hard to experience pain day
after day after day. So we keep busy and try to distract ourselves.

But our grief refuses to be hurried. It insists on taking as long
as it takes. It is a dawdler, a dilly-dallier, and a loafer.
That's its nature. There's simply no rushing it.

Here's the paradox, though. When we finally surrender to grief's
tortoise-like pace, we often find fast-acting relief. In slowing
down and accepting our grief's sluggishness, we may experience
a sudden sense of peace. We are aligning with what is
instead of what we wish would be.

*I respect my grief's slowness. It is going exactly
the speed it needs to go.*

OCTOBER 17

"Life is more fun if you play games."
— Roald Dahl

Love can be playful, right? We enjoy spending time on interesting and silly diversions with our loved ones. We also gently tease one another and try to make each other laugh. Some of the best parts of love are the fun and games.

So if grief is love's conjoined twin…shouldn't we try being playful in our grief sometimes as well? In grief, we're playful when we remind ourselves not to take everything so seriously. When we take time outs for fun and laughter. When we allow black humor to open the door to death and grief topics that our culture generally considers taboo.

I'm not sure I'd say that grief is more fun if you play games, but I would say that grief is more tolerable if you play games. It's also more true to life and love.

My grief has room for fun and laughter.

OCTOBER 18

"It is by going down into the abyss that we recover
the treasures of life."
— Joseph Campbell

Now *there's* a metaphor we can hold onto today: grief as a
dangerous, arduous treasure hunt. No, it's not a treasure hunt
we ever wanted to embark on, but here we are. And now
that we're in the abyss, shouldn't we look for the
treasure that's hidden here?

Because there *are* treasures to be found at the bottom of grief.
Like the shiny memories of joyous times spent with the person
who died. Like the golden realization that our lives are most
meaningful when we love and need other people. Like the
diamond clarity about what is truly important for us
to do and be from here on in.

When I am ready, I will become a treasure-seeker in my grief.

OCTOBER 19

*"Envy is the art of counting the other fellow's blessings
instead of your own."*

— Harold Coffin

We grievers can be an envious bunch. We've lost someone
important to us, yet we know many others who have not suffered
a similar loss. They go blithely about their lives, unaware of how
lucky they are to be able to experience what we no longer can.

It's normal and natural for loss to turn on the spotlight of envy.
"Look!" it says. "Look at what that person still has that we don't!"
Loss reveals not only our own "have-not" but the
corresponding "have" in others.

Of course, life isn't fair. Humans across the world enjoy and suffer
in wildly different measures. What's more, the very people we
are envying may be experiencing, unbeknownst to us,
their own profound losses and challenges.

We can work on cultivating perspective. We also can and should
express our envious thoughts and feelings, for they are our grief
talking. And grief is never right or wrong, honorable or shameful.
It just is. As always, giving our grief a voice outside of ourselves
helps us to befriend it, understand it, and, eventually,
reconcile ourselves to it.

*Any envy I might feel is part of my grief. It is normal
and natural and needs expression.*

OCTOBER 20

"I love deadlines. I like the whooshing sound they make as they fly by."
— Douglas Adams

What's our deadline for "getting over" this grief? Do we expect to be "back to normal" six months from now? A year? Two years?

Our culture wants it to happen as quickly as possible. The people around us would usually like us to hurry up, as well. We might even be self-imposing our own deadlines.

But grief doesn't work that way. It doesn't respond to timetables. It takes as long as it takes and in fact, never really ends

So the next time someone hints at a deadline for our grief, let's just smile and enjoy the sound of it whooshing by. We're masters enough of our own grief to realize by now that deadlines are mere sound effects.

My grief and healing have no deadlines. Their ideal pace is whatever pace they're going.

OCTOBER 21

"What a wonderful life I've had! I only wish I'd realized it sooner."
— Sidonie-Gabrielle Colette

We're dying, you and I. We're all of us dying, and sooner or later, our lives here on earth, too, will be over.

On our deathbeds, I suspect that our grief will shift. We'll have a newfound perspective. Not only will we have the forward-looking hope that we will soon be reunited with our precious people who have died, but we'll also have the backward-looking gratitude for the wonderful loves we were privileged to share.

I've sat at the deathbeds of several people I was close to, and while they expressed a range of thoughts and feelings, their predominant wish was to use their few remaining days to tell the stories of their lives. Those stories included the deaths of the people they loved, it's true, but mostly the stories focused on the *lives* of the people they loved and the time they got to spend together.

The dying have something to teach us about grieving.

Today and tomorrow and the day after, I will try
to realize what a wonderful life I have.

OCTOBER 22

"She experienced a moment of incandescent wonder, a sense of being connected, not just to these people, but to everyone and everything alive: every beating heart, every fluttering wing, every green shoot thrusting itself up out of the earth, seeking, as she was, the sun."
— Hillary Jordan

We *want* to feel connected to our lives here on earth. We *want* to feel the wonder of love and life. Trouble is, our feeling of disconnectedness from the person who died is often stronger.

In deep grief we experience the tug of loss more powerfully than the pull of life. This is normal and natural. We must learn to come to terms with and accommodate the loss before we can turn our faces to the sun.

We are connected to everyone and everything alive, though I also believe we are connected to everyone who has died. Saying yes to opportunities to strengthen and expand our feelings of connectedness helps us not only to survive our grief— it prepares the soil of our lives for richer days ahead.

I am connected to everyone and everything.

OCTOBER 23

*"Loneliness expresses the pain of being alone,
and solitude expresses the glory of being alone."*
— Paul Tillich

The loneliness of being without someone, especially someone who had been a part of our daily lives, is especially hard to cope with. As human beings we generally depend on companionship. When our companion is taken from us, our everyday routines are ripped in two.

Loneliness hurts. To counteract our loneliness, we must find ways to reach out to others. We can establish new routines of spending time with friends, family members, neighbors, fellow volunteers, work colleagues, likeminded hobbyists, and other people with whom we have things in common. Not only does working on connection quell our loneliness, it also provides us with listening ears for the expression of our grief.

But solitude is also necessary in grief. We need the stillness of alone time to feel our feelings and think our thoughts. To slow down and to turn inward, we must sometimes cultivate solitude. Being alone is not the curse we may have been making it out to be. It is actually a blessing. After all, we are born alone, and will die alone. We are each by ourselves a child of God.

*I will work on both connecting with others
and being OK with solitude.*

OCTOBER 24

"You can close your eyes to the things you don't want to see, but you can't close your heart to the things you don't want to feel."

— Johnny Depp

Our hearts are wise. They know our deepest truths.

When we don't want to feel our grief, we may be able to distract ourselves for a time. We can numb ourselves. We can deny. Such evasions are necessary for our survival sometimes, but they are always temporary measures.

Because we let love in, our hearts now experience grief. We opened our hearts to love, and so we cannot close them to grief. The grief lives inside our hearts alongside the love. The work that lies before us now is the day-by-day, week-by-week, month-by-month, year-by-year befriending of our grief.

Acknowledge it, embrace it, accommodate it, express it, and reconcile it we must.

I cannot close my heart to my grief. It's already in there, demanding my attention.

OCTOBER 25

"There are two kinds of people. One kind, you can just tell by looking at them at what point they congealed into their final selves. Whereas, the other kind keeps moving, changing… They are fluid. They keep moving forward and making new trysts with life, and the motion of it keeps them young. In my opinion, they are the only people who are still alive. You must be constantly on your guard against congealing."

— Gail Godwin

Some people get congealed in grief. Someone who means the world to them dies…and they get stuck. They become mired in the mud of their loss, and they sit down and give up.

Now don't get me wrong. It's normal and necessary for all of us to wallow in our grief for a while. The only way out is through. We have to feel it to heal it.

But two things prevent us from congealing: actively expressing our grief and nurturing our hope. Mourning is grief in motion. It's the motion that prevents the wet concrete of our grief from hardening us into place. And nurturing our hope means trying our darnedest to believe that good and loving things await us in our futures.

Mourning and hoping—they keep us truly alive.

*I do not want to congeal in grief, so I will keep moving.
I will actively mourn, and I will actively hope.*

OCTOBER 26

*"Don't be discouraged. It's often the last key in the bunch
that opens the lock."*

— Author Unknown

We can think of the actions we take to express our grief—
or mourn—as keys on a giant key ring. We encounter
a locked door, and we try a key.

Let's say the door that's blocking our way today is anger. We're
so mad—at the person who died, at the circumstances of the
death, at ourselves, etc. It's normal and necessary for us to feel
our anger if it keeps coming up for us, but we also need to
express it outside ourselves. So we try fitting one of the
keys on our key ring into the lock.

Maybe the first key we try is labeled "scream." We go into a
private room and we rage and yell our anger out loud for as
long as we feel like it. Then we see how we feel. If we're still
really angry, we might try other keys, such as those labeled
"journal" or "art." If our anger starts to soften, if the locked door
starts to open, we know we've found a key that works for us,
at least for today.

*My key ring is full of keys. Every day I'm going to try to find
the keys that open today's locks.*

OCTOBER 27

"Give crayons. Adults are disturbingly impoverished of these magical dream sticks."
— Dr. SunWolf

Let's always, always keep in mind that grief in motion is grief on the way to healing. Drawing, coloring, and creating art of any kind are all ways to put our grief into motion.

Have you been following the adult coloring book craze? You can now choose from hundreds of coloring books in different styles depicting myriad subjects. The idea is that the process of coloring in a pleasing and often complicated design is calming. It requires mindfulness. It's essentially a form of meditation.

Especially if you're someone who has ever liked to draw, doodle, or color, I encourage you to pick up an adult coloring book and give it a try. You may find the gentle, repetitive physical motion entrancing. The magical dream sticks just might transport you and your grief to a more peaceful place.

I think I'll try coloring (or drawing, playing with modeling clay, painting, etc.) today as a way to give motion to my grief.

OCTOBER 28

*"Sometimes, when one person is missing,
the whole world seems depopulated."*

— Lamartine

The French don't say, "I miss you." They say, *"Tu me manques,"*
which means, "You are missing from me."

The people we love are a part of us, and when they die, they
go missing from us. That's why we often say that whenever
someone special dies, a part of us dies, too.

This sensation of something essential now being missing in our
lives is the hardest part of our grief to learn to bear. It will never
go away. We cannot fill the hole with other people,
activities, or belongings. It's unfillable.

Yet maybe we can come to an understanding about the hole:
It is now a container for our memories and love for the person
who died. And while the memories and the love are not
a substitute for the person's presence, they, too,
are priceless beyond measure.

You are missing from me. I am learning to live with the hole.

OCTOBER 29

"I am learning every day to allow the space between where I am and where I want to be to inspire me and not terrify me."
— Tracee Ellis Ross

We're here, and we know that feeling better is way over there, on the other side of the grand canyon of our grief.

There's a big space between us and healing. Knowing that can make us feel discouraged, depressed, and afraid.

But we can see it as a challenge, instead, that canyon. It's never a challenge we'd choose; we'd rather have our special people back here with us. Since that's not possible, though, we can learn to think of our grief as an opportunity.

The journey's gonna be rough, but it's also gonna change us. Maybe we can look forward to meeting the us that we will have become on the other side of that canyon.

My grief is a grand canyon, but I'm feeling inspired to get to the other side.

OCTOBER 30

"We all wear masks, and the time comes when we cannot remove them without removing some of our own skin."
— André Berthiaume

Most of us grievers get good at wearing masks. Our culture tells us we need to "buck up," "keep it together," and "move forward," and so we go about our day-to-day lives doing what needs to be done, all the while wearing a mask that belies our true thoughts and feelings.

But here's the thing: We don't have to be different people on the outside than we are on the inside. We can be honest about our true thoughts and feelings. Healing our grief requires expressing it openly and honestly.

Let's take off our masks and stuff them in the closet today, even if it feels scary. Watch what happens.

Especially when I'm around friends and family today, I'm going to intentionally take off my mask.

OCTOBER 31

"Do you not know that a man is not dead
while his name is still spoken?"
— Terry Pratchett

In Mexico and other parts of the world, while we here in the United States are partaking in Halloween festivities on October 31st, millions of people are celebrating *Día de Muertos*, or Day of the Dead—a holiday that begins today but lasts for three days. Families build altars to their dead loved ones and visit their graves, bringing favorite foods, drinks, photos and memorabilia, and special decorations as gifts. The idea is to encourage the souls of the departed loved ones to visit the living during this time so that the living and dead can communicate.

How wonderful for entire communities and cultures to spend three days every year acknowledging loss and ritualizing the reality of undying love!

We don't have to live in a community that celebrates Day of the Dead to remember our departed loved ones. We can create our own daily, sporadic, or special occasion/holiday rituals to remember them and affirm our continued love for them. After all, Day of the Dead is every day in our hearts.

I will speak the name of my dead loved ones and
find ways to regularly remember them.

NOVEMBER 1

"In the book of Genesis, darkness was first. Light came second."
— Barbara Brown Taylor

In this darkening time of the year, I am reminded of the need for darkness in grief.

After the death of someone we love, the dark night of the soul can be a long and very black night indeed. It is uncomfortable and scary. It hurts. Yet if we allow ourselves to sit still in the blackness—without trying to fight it, deny it, or run away from it—we will find that it has something to teach us.

Befriending the darkness of grief takes courage and hard work. But it is only in doing so that we will eventually be able to reenter the light.

In grief, darkness is an essential step on the way to light.

NOVEMBER 2

"The boundaries which divide Life and Death are at best shadowy
and vague. Who shall say where the one ends and
where the other begins?"

— Edgar Allan Poe

In the Celtic tradition, "thin places" are spots where the separation between the physical world and the spiritual world seems most tenuous. They are places where the veil between Heaven and Earth, between the holy and the everyday, are so thin that when we are near them, we intuitively sense the timeless, boundless spiritual world.

Thin places are usually outdoors, often where water and land meet or land and sky come together. We might find thin places on a riverbank, a beach, or a mountaintop. Sacred spots—such as cathedrals, mosques, temples, memorials, cemeteries—are also often thin places. But really, wherever you feel a sense of otherworldly transcendence is a thin place for you, though it may not be for me.

Where do you feel closest to the person who died? Go there.

When I stumble across a thin place, I will take note…
and I will return there often.

NOVEMBER 3

"Depression is nourished by a lifetime of ungrieved
and unforgiven hurts."

— Penelope Sweet

Whenever we experience losses in life, we feel the hurt inside
us. We grieve. But unless we explore and express those griefs
outside of ourselves—in other words, unless we mourn—we
end up carrying the hurt forever. And in the carrying, the hurt
transmutes into difficulties with trust and intimacy, depression,
anxiety, substance abuse or other addictions,
and/or physical unwellness.

Carried grief squelches us. It extinguishes our divine sparks.

The good news is that it is never too late to mourn old griefs.
Through recalling and embracing long-buried feelings, we can
step forward into a joyful aliveness we never thought possible.

I so want to live my best life. I will work toward uncovering
and mourning all my carried griefs.

NOVEMBER 4

"Love yourself enough to set boundaries. Your time and energy are precious. You get to choose how to use it. You teach people how to treat you by deciding what you will and won't accept."

— Anna Taylor

Setting boundaries in grief is often necessary to our healing.

First, we have to set boundaries with other people, particularly those who judge us for our grief, make us feel ashamed, or engage in behaviors we know to be detrimental to our healing. We can simply choose not to spend time with them.

Second, we have to set boundaries with our jobs and other obligations. Our time and energy are precious. We need both to befriend and express our grief. We must be assertive in prioritizing time for self-care.

And third, we have to set boundaries with ourselves. We must guard against self-destructive behaviors as well as any potential tendencies we might have to "stuff" our grief, over-intellectualize our grief, or spurn the help and involvement of others who care about us.

I love myself and want healing enough for myself to set boundaries.

NOVEMBER 5

"If your compassion does not include yourself, it is incomplete."
— Buddha

Many of us are good at being kind to others yet pretty bad at being kind to ourselves. If there's one habit we need to break during our time of grief, it's this one.

We must be gentle with ourselves when we are grieving. We must be kind and self-forgiving. We must love ourselves unconditionally. After all, we are torn apart and need good care to heal.

The word "compassion" means "with passion." Let's care for ourselves with passion—physically, cognitively, emotionally, socially, and spiritually. And let's let others care for us with passion too.

Today and tomorrow and all the rest of the days,
I will care for myself with passion.

NOVEMBER 6

"Grief lasts longer than sympathy, which is one of the tragedies of the grieving."
— Elizabeth McCracken

Grief is usually quick to arrive but slow to heal. Even when we are anticipating the loss of a loved one who is ill, when they die the sudden force of our grief can knock us over. From there it lasts as long as it lasts. The most painful phase may take months or years.

When our grief seems slow, we must be patient. At the same time, we often find that actively expressing it gives it momentum.

Most of our friends and family members who are not grieving can't stick with us for the duration of our grief. It takes too long and is too hard to be present to. But if we can find just one or two people who understand the ongoing need for us to share our grief over the long haul, that is enough.

I give my grief permission to take as long as it takes. If I ever feel stuck, I will work at expressing my grief in some way, which will help set it in motion again.

NOVEMBER 7

"Take my word for it, the saddest thing under the sky
is a soul incapable of sadness."

— Countess de Gasparin

It's hard for us to appreciate this right now, but sadness isn't the saddest thing in the world. The incapacity for sadness is.

We love; we lost; we grieve.

We are the lucky ones.

My sadness is a symptom of love. I am one of the fortunate.

NOVEMBER 8

"It's good to have an end to journey toward;
but it's the journey that matters, in the end."
— Ursula K. LeGuin

You've probably noticed that I often use the metaphor of a journey through the wilderness when talking about grief. It's true. Grief is not an event or even a short period of time. It's a long, drawn-out affair that takes you to the wilderness of your soul.

In grief, we're journeying toward healing. We're experiencing and expressing our grief as we move—sometimes forward, sometimes backward, sometimes in circles—toward the unseen destination of renewed hope and happiness (or what I call reconciliation).

It's good to have a destination to journey toward. But having mourned much in my own life and worked with many mourners, I also know that the journey through grief itself is often, with the benefit of hindsight, a rewarding, enriching experience. And so, let us try to live with gratitude as much as possible for our daily lives, even in grief.

I'm on a journey that is painful but also alive with possibilities.

NOVEMBER 9

"In one of the stars, I shall be living. In one of them, I shall be laughing. And so it will be as if all the stars were laughing when you look at the sky at night."

— Antoine de Saint Exupéry

Where are you?

I said goodbye to your body. It was you but not you. It was the part of you I could hold and smell, see and hear. Your body was precious to me because it animated you.

But you don't inhabit your body anymore. I could tell that immediately. So where did you go? And if you don't look like you anymore, how will I find you?

When those we love die, we often look to the heavens, imagining they somehow live "up there" now. The night skies can be a source of comfort and wonder. Our universe is mysterious and beautiful; it is so much larger and more complex than we can comprehend. The stars offer us solace and, if we let them, a kind of answer to our unanswerable questions.

I wish I could see where you've gone. For the time being, imagining is the next best thing.

NOVEMBER 10

"So often when we come upon a wall, we do not look around for an opening—the tunnel that leads to the other side, where we can walk on the cobblestone road of life and hold hands with love."
— Bridgette Rodriguez

Our grief is a kind of wall. It's tall and wide and seems insurmountable. On the other side of the wall lies healing and happiness, but we just don't see how we'll ever be able to get over the wall.

We *can't* get over the wall. We can only go through it. You see, there is an opening in our grief. It's a tunnel called mourning.

In this long, dark, and rocky tunnel, we find our way slowly forward by acknowledging, embracing, and expressing our grief. We cry in the tunnel. We tell our stories of love and loss in the tunnel. We share memories and reach out for help in the tunnel.

The light at the end of the tunnel is hope. It may be faint and far, far away, but it's there, pulling us forward.

The tunnel through the wall of my grief is mourning.

NOVEMBER 11

"Wabi-sabi nurtures all that is authentic by acknowledging three realities: nothing lasts, nothing is finished, nothing is perfect."
— Richard Powell

The Japanese concept of *wabi-sabi* embraces the imperfection and fleetingness of life. The philosophy also values simplicity and nature.

In life, nothing material lasts. Material goods come and go. Bodies are born and eventually die. And nothing is perfect. Even our love for and relationship with the person who died was flawed in countless ways.

Life is imperfect and fleeting. Maybe love, in all its imperfection, is the only thing that *does* last.

I am learning to appreciate the temporary and imperfect beauty of life.

NOVEMBER 12

"All great changes are preceded by chaos."
— Deepak Chopra

Our grief can feel so chaotic. It's like being in the middle
of a wild, rushing river with nothing to hold onto.
We're confused, befuddled, and disorganized.

It's dizzying and miserable.

But our chaos is rearranging us. We must trust that it is making
new patterns and connections. Over time, as we do our grief
work, we will eventually begin to see the changed yet
beautiful new us we are becoming.

I may never be someone who thrives on chaos,
but I can work to be someone who trusts in the
regenerative power of temporary chaos.

NOVEMBER 13

"Real love stories don't have endings."
— Gregory J.P. Godek

People die, but love does not.

Mourning the death and continuing to love the person who died are not mutually exclusive. Actually, integrating loss into our lives means having the courage to continue to love, even in the face of loss.

We could not stop loving even if we wanted to. Yet because the person we love is no longer here to receive our love, we must transform it into loving memory and eternal connectedness, carrying it with us for the rest of our lives—and beyond.

Now the quest becomes to travel through life still and always intertwined with the person who died yet open to new paths and relationships that will bring continued meaning to each of our days until we, too, vanish into the heavens.

My love story will continue forever.

NOVEMBER 14

"If you want to find the secrets of the universe, think in terms of energy, frequency, and vibration."

— Nikola Tesla

Prana is the Sanskrit word for "life force" or "life energy." The Chinese call it *chi* (also spelled *qi*). Various cultures and holistic disciplines, such as yoga, hold that our bodies harbor *pranic* waves, which give us energy and also connect us to the universal *prana* that binds everyone and everything in life together. *Prana* energy is the essence called upon in acupuncture, qigong, tai chi, meditation, and other traditional arts.

Here in the Western world, we use the term "spirit." Our spirits have been dulled and dampened by grief, which is why we use the phrase "low spirits" to describe sadness and depression. Nurturing our spirits and building them back up is our central goal on the path to healing.

The traditional arts mentioned above help us bolster our *prana*. So do getting enough rest, eating well, exercising appropriately, and partaking in activities that we find meaningful and joyful. As we mourn, we are well served to remember to nurture our spirits.

When my spirits are low, I will take this as a cue that I need to spend more time nurturing my spirit.

NOVEMBER 15

"Stress can destroy much more than just our physical health.
Too often, it eats away at our hope, belief, and faith."
— Charles F. Glassman

Stress comes from demand, challenge, and change. Our grief
is stressful. So are many circumstances in our lives.

We have to grieve right now. But we probably don't have to
engage with all of the other stress. It's sapping our capacity
for hope, belief, and faith.

Now's a good time to make a list of situations and activities we
often find stressful. How many of these can we eliminate
from our daily lives? Let's get started.

Today I will eliminate at least one stressful thing from my life.
If I feel guilty about it, I will remember that right now my hope,
belief, and faith are more important.

NOVEMBER 16

*"You don't heal from the loss of a loved one because time passes;
you heal because of what you do with the time."*
— Carol Crandall

Expecting time alone to heal our grief is kind of like expecting
time alone to get us in shape. It simply ain't gonna happen.

Working our bodies most days of every week is how we
achieve and maintain fitness. Likewise, working our grief—
acknowledging it, befriending it, and sharing it outside
ourselves in various ways, most days of every week—
is how we slowly move toward healing.

We've loved and lost. Now time stretches on before us.
Let's make the most of that time, so that we can heal
and live and love fully again.

*I've got grief work to do—today, tomorrow,
the next day, ad infinitum.*

NOVEMBER 17

"Something amazing happens when we surrender and just love. We melt into another world, a realm of power already within us. The world changes when we change. The world softens when we soften. The world loves us when we choose to love the world."

— Marianne Williamson

Eventually we come to realize that if we surrender to our loss, it slowly begins to exert less power over us. We muster the courage to turn our attention to it—to feel and experience it fully—and in doing so, we find that it loses some of its strength.

Surrendering to our grief takes more guts than fighting it. It is also more effective.

When we learn to meet our grief with love and acceptance, it softens. And all that is good and meaningful in the world opens up to us again.

I am working on surrendering to my grief.

NOVEMBER 18

*"Life is like music. It must be composed by ear,
feeling, and instinct, not by rule."*

— Samuel Butler

Have you noticed that grief is instinctual? No one has to teach us to feel pain, conjure memories of the person who died, and ponder the "whys" of life and death. All of these thoughts and feelings come to us naturally.

Mourning, on the other hand, is more culturally shaped. We learn what is OK to express and for how long. Society's rules for grief and mourning restrict the expression of our instinctual grief.

We're learning to ignore society's ridiculous rules, though. Whatever we instinctually think and feel inside, we will express outside without shame.

My grief is like music. It is composed by ear, feeling, and instinct, not by rules.

NOVEMBER 19

"Maybe there's something you're afraid to say, or someone you're afraid to love, or somewhere you're afraid to go. It's gonna hurt. It's gonna hurt because it matters."

— John Green

Our fears in grief teach us what matters. If we're afraid to live on alone, that teaches us that having a companion matters to us. If we're afraid of financial problems, that teaches us that financial stability matters to us. If we're afraid to tell others what we're really thinking and feeling inside, that teaches us that those thoughts and feelings matter to us.

We can use our fears to identify what is worth taking risks for in our continued living. Then we can embrace our fear and work through it, reaching out for the things that matter to us most.

We can also use our hurt to identify what matters. Whenever we hurt, that means we've lost something or someone. The hurt is a symptom of loss—and it teaches us what is important to us and what we must work toward remaking in our lives.

I'm going to work on not being afraid of fear and hurt because they are my teachers.

NOVEMBER 20

"The worst part of holding the memories is not the pain.
It's the loneliness of it. Memories need to be shared."

— Lois Lowry

Our memories often hurt us. It can be painful to remember the
person who died—the good times as well as the bad times—
because the memories so strongly evoke the person's absence
now as well as her absence for all the days of our future.

But from my own personal experience as well as from all my
decades of counseling mourners, I've learned that there comes
a time when we're ready to unpack the memories. If they're
happy memories, it's like we have a treasure inside us that needs
to be shared. It's lonely keeping all those memories to ourselves.
If they're more challenging memories, we begin to realize that
working through them will require sharing them. They'll
keep bothering us until we do.

The sharing of our memories causes us pain too, of course,
but it becomes a more bittersweet pain, with the sweet
outweighing the bitter a little more each time.

When I'm ready, I need to share my memories.

NOVEMBER 21

"When one is pretending, the entire body revolts."
— Anaïs Nin

Our grief is wily. It will try every means possible
to get our attention.

If we're ignoring, denying, or postponing our grief, it will often
turn to our bodies as a means of expression. It will
literally make us sick.

Aches and pains, viral illnesses, autoimmune diseases, even
cardiovascular and other systemic troubles often arise when
we're not giving our grief the attention and expression
it needs and deserves.

*My body's health is, in part, a reflection of the health
of my mourning.*

NOVEMBER 22

"You don't have a soul. You are a soul. You have a body."
— C.S. Lewis

We are timeless souls. Not everyone believes this, but the idea is at least something to ponder.

If our souls came down to earth to inhabit these bodies, they will continue on after our bodies are done living. Thrillingly, this would also mean that the souls of our loved ones whose bodies have died are also—at this very moment— living on somehow, somewhere.

I believe that grief is the soul's journey through earthly loss. Here in this temporal existence, our souls are touched by what it means to be human. And so they grieve. Mourning allows our souls to fully experience and express their human existence, creating hope and meaning for all the days we have left on this beautiful blue planet.

I don't have a soul. I am a soul. My soul is crying out for me to express my grief.

NOVEMBER 23

"The unthankful heart…discovers no mercies; but let the thankful heart sweep through the day and, as the magnet finds the iron, so it will find, in every hour, some heavenly blessings!"
— Henry Ward Beecher

It is hard to be thankful this year. There is so much to grieve, so much to mourn. There is crushing loss, and that dreaded empty seat at the table.

Yet the paradox: it is the thankful heart that attracts mercy. We need comfort and care this season. We need mercy. Only the tender heart that we keep open to feeling and expressing grief as well as gratitude is open to mercy.

And so we grieve and have gratitude both. We grasp the door to our heart that can trap our pain inside and prevent mercy and care from entering, and we tear it off its hinges. We leave the opening open. Pain goes out; blessings come in.

My heart is unthankful for the loss but thankful for so much else. I will allow both to sweep through this day.

NOVEMBER 24

"In November, the earth is growing quiet. It is making its bed, a winter bed for flowers and small creatures. The bed is white and silent, and much life can hide beneath its blankets."

— Cynthia Rylant

When we grow quiet in our grief, we are making a winter bed for necessary withdrawal and stillness. We instinctively yearn for solitude, and so, like turtles, we pull ourselves inside our shells and grieve in isolation.

Yet much life can hide beneath our stillness. We are remembering, thinking, and feeling. We are going to the wilderness of our own souls, and along the way, we are doing the necessary work of reviewing everything that has happened.

After a period of quiet, it will once again be time to emerge and share our grief with our community. But for now, hush. We are settling in.

I sometimes crave withdrawal and stillness.
The winter of my grief calls to me.

NOVEMBER 25

"It's so curious: one can resist tears and 'behave' very well in the hardest hours of grief. But then someone makes you a friendly sign behind a window, or one notices that a flower that was in bud only yesterday has suddenly blossomed, or a letter slips from a drawer... and everything collapses. "

— Sidonie-Gabrielle Colette

We can be so surprisingly tender in our grief. The smallest, most harmless, everyday thing can pierce our hearts like a needle.

It's because our hearts are wounded. They are injured, and the wounds are easily pained.

The surprising moments of pain call us to attend to our grief. "I'm still here!" our grief says. "I still need your attention!"

When something simple pricks my heart with pain, I will know that I need to take a moment to mourn. I will know that the pain is a signal for me to slow down and embrace my grief.

NOVEMBER 26

"Give thanks for unknown blessings already on their way."
— Native American Saying

At Thanksgiving we do a sort of backward-looking inventory.
We consider that which we have had the privilege of
experiencing in the past as well as in the present, and we say
thank you—to each other and to God.

This is a lovely, meaningful tradition, but let us also consider
that giving thanks may at any time also be a forward-looking
expectation. We can choose to anticipate blessings that are
sure to come our way. We can, in other words,
cultivate hope and faith.

Good things are already on their way to us. I believe this,
and I hope you do too.

I give thanks for the good that is yet to be in my life.

NOVEMBER 27

"We can only be said to be alive in those moments when our hearts are conscious of our treasures."

— Thornton Wilder

After we survive the early days and weeks of our grief, this is our goal, isn't it? To truly live the rest of our days. To be really and fully alive even as we continue to mourn.

Our aliveness, says Wilder, depends on our mindful awareness of the gifts in our lives. And so we strive to live in the moment and to have gratitude for those we love and all our many treasures.

Our love for the person who died was—and is—one of those treasures. When we find the courage to give thanks for that love, we are really and fully alive.

Today I give thanks for the person who died. I give thanks for the love we shared and the love I still feel.

NOVEMBER 28

"Some foods are so comforting, so nourishing of body and soul, that to eat them is to be home again after a long journey. To eat such a meal is to remember that, though the world is full of knives and storms, the body is built for kindness."

— Eli Brown

For many of us, our appetites have been affected by our grief. Some of us aren't hungry, while others of us may be overeating in response to the stress.

While we can't eat (or not eat) our troubles away, we can now and then turn to sensory pleasures for comfort and even healing. If we have comfort foods, now is the time to enjoy them in moderation. I myself love tucking in to a generous bowl of spaghetti. It reminds me of my German father, who loved to say, "I'm a German who thinks he is Italian" as he went back for his third plate. I remember him fondly as, in tribute to him, I do the same.

Our bodies are indeed built for kindness. Giving them things they find pleasurable helps us find moments of enjoyment in the midst of our grief and reconstruct reasons for living.

My favorite food is _____.
I'll treat myself to some today.

NOVEMBER 29

"I have been driven many times upon my knees by the overwhelming conviction that I had nowhere else to go. My own wisdom and that of all about me seemed insufficient for that day."

— Abraham Lincoln

When we have nowhere else to go, many of us are driven to our knees—literally or figuratively—in prayer. Prayers about grief are mourning, you know. They are a form of expressing your grief outside yourself, of trying to communicate your grief to someone else.

We are so very tiny in this universe. Our lives are infinitesimal specks. In that context, we are utterly powerless and without wisdom.

But maybe God will share a morsel of his wisdom with us if we only ask. Perhaps sharing our grievous thoughts and feelings with him will be just the outpouring we need to make room for more hopeful thoughts and feelings today. Let's try.

Dear God, I have so many things to say and to ask.
I trust you are listening.

NOVEMBER 30

*"You have not lived a perfect day…unless you have done something
for someone who will never be able to pay you back."*
— Ruth Smeltzer

What's a perfect day in grief, anyway? I would say it's a day in
which we've embraced and expressed any thoughts and feelings
that came up, been honest with—as well as kind to—ourselves
and others, and tried to appreciate each moment.

But maybe Ruth Smeltzer is right. Maybe our perfect day is not
truly perfect unless we've also gone out of our way to actively
help someone who can't pay us back. Who maybe
doesn't even deserve it.

Grief is an appropriately me-focused experience. But when
we're ready, looking around us each day for an opportunity to
be of service to someone else can turbo-charge our healing.
If we serve selflessly, we end up saving ourselves.

*When I am ready and have the energy to help others,
I will start looking for small, daily opportunities.*

DECEMBER 1

*"I would rather be ashes than dust! I would rather that my spark
burn out in a brilliant blaze than it be stifled by dry-rot. I would
rather be a superb meteor, every atom of me in magnificent glow,
than a sleepy and permanent planet. The function of man is to live,
not to exist. I shall not waste my days trying to prolong them.
I shall use my time."*

— Jack London

Who is not stirred by such a sentiment? Fortunately for us
mourners, its message applies just as much in times of grief
as it does in times of boredom or joy.

To live in grief is to reach out to others, to talk about our
thoughts and feelings, to sob, to journal, to express. To use
our grieving time is to mourn actively, openly, and fully.

So let's not waste too many of our days in denial and distraction.
Let's be bold. Let's be meteors in grief, our inner truths
brilliantly ablaze for everyone to see.

I want to live, not just exist. I shall use my time of grieving.

DECEMBER 2

"I used to trouble about what life was for. Now being alive seems sufficient reason."
— Joanna Field

What were the lives of our loved ones who died for? Did they have some grand purpose here on earth, or have we realized that it was a miracle that they simply lived?

We may never come to a satisfactory conclusion about what life is for. But being alive—there are myriad day-to-day joys and moments of meaning in that.

Just think: We are alive. Our loved ones were alive, and we were fortunate to have our lives intersect with theirs. What an amazing gift.

I am working on feeling grateful for life.

DECEMBER 3

"If we want to avoid the suffering of leaving, we will never experience the joy of loving. And love is stronger than fear, life stronger than death, hope stronger than despair. We have to trust that the risk of loving is always worth taking."
— Henri Nouwen

We have come to know the consequences of loving. We have loved and lost. And so we must now grieve.

And yet, even in our moments of deepest pain, we harbor a profound knowing: It was worth it. Without a doubt, we would do it all over again. Of course we would!

Paradoxically, the love we were privileged to experience is the only thing that prevents the heaviness of our grief from crushing us. It is both the cause and the cure, the problem and the solution. It is love that will sustain and ultimately renew us.

Was it worth it? I will ask myself this question, and the answer will help see me through.

DECEMBER 4

*"Have you ever lost someone you love and wanted one more conver-
sation, one more chance to make up for the time when you thought
they would be here forever? If so, then you know you can go your
whole life collecting days, and none will outweigh the one
you wish you had back."*

— Mitch Albom

Oh how we wish for one more conversation, one more hug,
one more chance to say, "I love you so, so much."

We look back at our time together and see missed opportunities.
How foolish we were! How complacent! How oblivious
to the miracle right in front of us!

And yet, we were and are simply human. We did our silly
best then, and we're doing our silly best now. We are perfectly
imperfect, deserving of unconditional self-love and
self-forgiveness. Such is life.

Maybe, though, we can take what we're learning from this grief
experience and apply to it to our relationships with people
who are still living. Now *there's* an opportunity.

I've learned essential things from my grief that I can use today.

DECEMBER 5

"Everyone must leave something behind when he dies, my grandfather said. A child or a book or a painting or a house or a wall built or a pair of shoes made. Or a garden planted. Something your hand touched some way so your soul has somewhere to go when you die, and when people look at that tree or that flower you planted, you're there."

— Ray Bradbury

Our loved ones who died devoted time and energy to various passions. They made, collected, or nurtured things—objects, hobbies, places, relationships with pets and people. Wherever they laid their hands with love, those places are sacred.

After my father died, I placed photos of him in a place where I would see them often. I surrounded the photos with things that connected me to him, such as his tennis racket and a favorite baseball cap. This became a sacred place where I could stop and mourn, remember, share my memories with others, and heal.

The concept of psychometry holds that people leave behind vibrational imprints on objects they've touched or places they've lived. Followers believe that touching or holding these objects or spending time in these places allows us to connect with those who have died not just through memory but in a more physical, literal way. I know that when I wear my father's watch, I feel his presence.

Today I will touch something my loved one cherished or spend time in a place where part of his soul still resides.

DECEMBER 6

"Optimist: Someone who figures that taking a step backward after taking a step forward is not a disaster, it's a cha-cha."

— Robert Brault

Grief is often a one step forward, two steps back kind of a journey. It's also a going in circles and sometimes getting lost kind of a journey. It's frustrating, but like all of life, it's also how it is.

We can choose to be optimists or pessimists in grief. Optimists find ways to foster hope for the future and trust that the journey—no matter how challenging—is taking them toward healing. We still experience pain. We still get lost and angry and depressed. But even in the midst of our necessary suffering, we try very hard to nurture the knowing that our lives can and will continue with meaning and love.

The next time we take a step—or two or three or fifty-seven— backward, let's remember that grief is a dance, and if we only keep dancing, we're doing what we need to do.

Today I reaffirm my intention to be an optimist in grief.

DECEMBER 7

"We don't receive wisdom; we must discover it for ourselves after a journey that no one can take for us or spare us."

— Marcel Proust

We grow wiser on our journey through grief, but it is wisdom we work hard for. We definitely earn it.

If we could live our lives without ever experiencing loss, we would choose such a joyful existence over wisdom. But alas, this is an impossibility. What's more, no one can take our losses away from us or spare us from them.

And so we lose, and we grow wise. Along the way, the more we embrace and express our grief, the wiser—and ultimately more renewed—we become.

Today I will pause to take stock of the wisdom I have earned. What do I know is true, and how can I use this wisdom to make the most of my days left on earth?

DECEMBER 8

"There's a fine edge to new grief. It severs nerves, disconnects reality—there's mercy in a sharp blade. Only with time, as the edge wears, does the real ache begin."

— Christopher Moore

New grief is characterized by numbness. We simply cannot absorb all at once the full reality of what happened and what it means. We feel disoriented, confused, and foggy. Our shock protects us for a while.

Over time, as we begin to understand the fact of the death not only with our heads but with our hearts, the real ache sets it.

Seeing grief as our friend instead of our foe helps us survive through the deepening pain. It hurts, yes, but it is a normal and necessary hurt. Welcoming it and exploring it, in fact, is the very process that eventually eases it.

I am aching, but it is a normal and necessary ache.

DECEMBER 9

*"She was no longer wrestling with the grief, but could sit down with it
as a lasting companion and make it a sharer in her thoughts."*
— George Eliot

Our grief will soften, but it will be with us forever. Since it
is now a permanent part of our lives, we have a choice:
We can consider it an enemy or a friend.

Treating our grief as an enemy means disliking it, wrestling with
it, and avoiding it. Treating is as a friend means welcoming it,
paying attention to it, and holding it close.

When we sit down with our grief as a lasting companion, we
surrender to the truth that like its twin, love, grief teaches us
what is most important and, if we allow it to, always offers wise
counsel. Far from an enemy, grief is a BFF. Who'd have thought?

My grief is a lasting and trusted companion.

DECEMBER 10

*"He who waits to do a great deal of good at once
will never do anything."*
— Samuel Johnson

In my work as a grief counselor and educator, I've encountered
people who seemed to be "saving up" their grief work. They've
been putting it off. They've procrastinated acknowledging,
befriending, and expressing their grief. Most days, they're
keeping themselves busy in an effort to avoid,
repress, or deny their grief.

"One day I'll deal with it," they tell themselves. The trouble is, of
course, that day never comes. Besides, one big mourning
day could never be nearly enough.

Mourning is a daily, incremental practice that slowly and over
time moves us toward healing. It simply can't be done all at
once. The grief we feel inside is different each day, and it's that
day's unique grief that needs to be expressed.

*Like the internal experience of grief, the external expression
that is mourning is a daily practice. It's a way of life.*

DECEMBER 11

"Make the most of your regrets; never smother sorrow, but tend and cherish it 'til it comes to have a separate and integral interest. To regret deeply is to live afresh."

— Henry David Thoreau

Just as we are tending and cherishing our grief in general, we can choose to tend and cherish any regrets that may be part of our grief.

Cherishing regrets seems like a paradox, right? Yet I think Thoreau is profoundly correct. Devoting the time and energy to feel and explore our regrets—welcoming them as dear friends instead of shunning them as enemies—allows us to better understand what we really care about. The deeper a regret, the more important the value it is tethered to.

To regret deeply is to be given the chance to learn and grow. It is to be graced with the opportunity to live afresh.

I welcome my regrets as dear friends because they have essential lessons to teach me.

DECEMBER 12

*"Sometimes we get through adversity only by imagining what the
world might be like if our dreams should ever come true."*
— Arthur Golden

We have a dream these days. In our dream, we have our special
person back—here on earth, with us. Unfortunately, that is
the one dream that cannot ever come true.

We can also dream about what our lives will be like again when
we are not consumed by grief every day. In this dream, we
are content and appreciative of life. We experience joy
and laughter, love and connection.

This second dream is possible. It is the life that awaits us on the
other side of the hard work of mourning. In that life, the wound
of our grief has healed, though it has left behind a scar that
we will carry forever. Believing in this second dream
fosters hope and healing.

*Today there may be adversity, but in my tomorrows
I imagine happiness and meaning.*

DECEMBER 13

"What happens when you let go, when your strength leaves you and you sink into darkness, when there's nothing that you can or anyone else can do, no matter how desperate you are, no matter how you try? Perhaps it's then, when you have neither pride nor power, that you are saved, brought to an unimaginably great reward."

— Mark Halperin

People tell us that we have to let go of the person who died. They tell us that we have to let go of our grief.

Not possible. Can't be done. They are both part of us, forever.

What we can—what we must—let go of is our need to control our grief. When we let ourselves go to our grief, when we surrender to it, when we relinquish our pride and our illusions of power and fully experience and express whatever we are thinking and feeling, we are saved.

I will let myself go to my grief. In surrendering, I will be saved.

DECEMBER 14

"The idea is to find some bit of holiness in everything—food, sex, earning and spending money, having children, conversations with friends. Everything can be seen as a miracle, as part of God's plan. When we can truly see this, we nourish our souls."

— Rabbi Harold S. Kushner

If we look—if we really look—what bits of holiness could we find today?

I glance around me at this very moment and I see the lovely branches of the evergreen trees outside my window. I see the photos of my family. I see my hands, challenged by osteoarthritis but still nimble and capable. I see the cozy space that shelters me as I write every day.

Our lives may be bittersweet, but they are also miraculous.

I will look for bits of holiness today and when I spot them, I will say a silent word of gratitude.

DECEMBER 15

"I have lived with you and loved you, and now you are gone. Gone where I cannot follow, until I have finished all of my days."

— Victoria Hanley

I miss you.

I miss you.

I miss you.

I cannot follow you, and you cannot return to me.

Our separation is excruciating. I cannot imagine bearing it until I have finished all of my days. But know this: When I have finished all of my days, it is my most sacred intention to find you again.

I will miss you until I have finished all of my days.

DECEMBER 16

"Ten years, she's dead, and I still find myself some mornings reaching for the phone to call her. She could no more be gone than gravity or the moon."

— Mary Karr

That initial shock and numbness we experienced when we first learned of the death—it never totally goes away. Years later, we still find ourselves thinking that the person who died could walk through the door at any moment.

Over time, we mostly come to terms with their gone-ness, but never 100 percent. A part of our hearts and minds seems unable to truly believe it. At times, I still wish and wait for my dad to walk through the door and back into my life.

Maybe the part of us that still clings to the impossibility of the death is right. Maybe it's the part that knows that death is but an illusion. Something to ponder for today, anyway.

Sometimes I still can't believe that you're gone.

DECEMBER 17

*"Live as if you were to die tomorrow. Learn as if
you were to live forever."*
— Mahatma Gandhi

Sometimes when we're grieving we wish we would die. I'm
not talking about actively planning suicide. I'm talking about
passive, passing thoughts in which we wish we could escape
our misery. This is normal and natural. (Active suicidal thoughts
and planning, on the other hand, require immediate help.)

So let's pretend for a minute that we knew we would die
tomorrow. What would we do today? What would we definitely
not do? Who would we spend time with? Who would
we reach out to?

Now let's pretend that we knew we would live forever. (For
imagination's sake, let's also pretend we didn't have to worry
about money.) What would we want to explore? What's on
our no-holds-barred bucket list?

*Today I will strive to live as if I were going to die tomorrow,
and I will also embark on learning something new as if
I knew I were going to live forever.*

DECEMBER 18

"Gifts of grace come to all of us. But we must be ready to see and willing to receive these gifts. It will require a kind of sacrifice, the sacrifice of believing that, however painful our losses, life can still be good— good in a different way than before, but nevertheless good."

— Gerald L. Sittser

In the beginning, we're often not ready and willing to receive gifts of grace. We're too smothered by the darkness of our loss. We're appropriately wallowing in and befriending our pain, and we're not yet prepared to acknowledge glimmers of goodness and hope.

But over time, to actively mourn is to open our eyes to goodness and hope. We have to work to cultivate grace. It is not a passive achievement; it is an accomplishment borne of effort and sacrifice.

Our lives can be good again—good in a different way than before, but still good.

I am ready and willing to receive the gifts of grace.

DECEMBER 19

*"The holiest of holidays are those kept by ourselves in silence
and apart: The secret anniversaries of the heart."*
— Henry Wadsworth Longfellow

We grievers treasure memories of certain moments with our
loved ones who died, such as the first time we met, the day we
visited a special place together, the specific time and location we
heard important news. Often these secret anniversaries of the
heart are as or more precious to us than birthdays and popular
holidays. They are the private, touchstone memories
that glow with the essence of our love.

Often these holiest of holidays cannot be adequately captured
in words. Telling others about them or writing them down on
paper falls flat. Symbols and rituals, however, are sometimes
powerful enough to help us honor them appropriately.

We can create a small display—such as a shadowbox, mini-tree
to decorate, wall shrine, or tabletop still life—of objects and
mementos associated with our secret anniversaries. We can
also ritualize our holy holidays by spending the day revisiting
special places or repeating certain activities. When words are
inadequate, such symbols and rituals help us embrace
and express our most profound grief.

**I treasure my secret anniversaries and will
look for ways to honor them.**

DECEMBER 20

"Even in darkness, it is possible to create light."
— Elie Wiesel

The darkness of our grief, especially during the dark parts of the year, can overwhelm us with despair.

While befriending the darkness is an essential part of our grief work, so is creating sparks of light. We must dose ourselves with the darkness then actively find or create ways to pluck up moments of levity, connection, happiness, and joy.

Even in our darkest nights of grief, we can create light. We can call a friend. We can share a bowl of popcorn with a loved one while we watch a comedy movie together. We can Skype with someone far away. We can take a bubble bath, eat our favorite foods, get a massage, read a book we enjoy—anything that gives us a momentary spark of peace or pleasure.

Even in the darkness of my grief, it is necessary to create and grab hold of light.

DECEMBER 21

"In a dark time, the eye begins to see."

- Theodore Roethke

During these darkest days of the year, we often find ourselves struggling with our darkest emotions—sadness, emptiness, loss, depression, despair, shame, and fear.

The winter of our grief is often long and cold.

But we must learn to see the darkness as our friend. In fact, it is in befriending our pain that we learn from it and unlock our capacity to be transformed by it. Our dark emotions are not bad; they simply *are*. When we are feeling them, that means we *need* to feel them. We must muster the courage to explore and experience them to the full. Only then will they soften and fade, clearing a space for new love and joy.

Darkness is my friend. When it knocks,
I will open the door and embrace it.

DECEMBER 22

"The meaning of life is to find your gift.
The purpose of life is to give it away."
— Pablo Picasso

In this gift-giving season, let us consider the gifts we were
born with or cultivated during our lives.

I am someone who believes that some people have callings.
Mine is to help people mourn well so they can live and
love well again. Do you have a calling?

Even if you don't have a calling, you have unique gifts. You
brought your gifts into your relationship with the person who
died. Now that this person is no longer here to receive your
gifts, what can you do with them? You can give
them away to others.

Being your unique self in relationship to others is your purpose.
Remember: Expressing yourself is mourning, which is how you
heal. Whenever you are expressing your authentic self, even if a
particular expression is not directly "about" your grief, you
are mourning—because genuineness can't help but
reveal the whole of you.

***In giving my gifts away to others, I am being true
to myself and to my grief.***

DECEMBER 23

"What is Christmas? It is tenderness for the past, courage for the present, hope for the future. It is a fervent wish that every cup may overflow with blessings rich and eternal, and that every path may lead to peace."

— Agnes M. Pahro

We are tender this Christmas. We despair at the thought of the now-empty chair at our holiday table—whether it is an actual chair or an empty space in our hearts. It is too painful a reminder that someone we love is gone forever.

We may decide that leaving the chair empty is the best way to honor our grief this holiday season. Or we may decide to fill our empty chair. Maybe we could invite a friend or neighbor to our holiday gathering. Perhaps we could reach out to someone else touched by this death. Together we could acknowledge the person who is missing while at the same time finding solace in each other's company.

If we acknowledge, embrace, and express our grief this holiday, we are on the path that leads to peace.

Your empty chair grieves me. My Christmas heart is tender. I will remember and mourn you today.

DECEMBER 24

"Christmas is a time when you get homesick—even when you're home."
— Carol Nelson

When someone we love has died, the holidays can be so very painful. The heart of the holidays has been torn apart. Without love, what is life? Without the people we love, what are the holidays?

Yet the holidays also offer us the healing power of ritual. We created holiday rituals in the first place because everyday activities and normal conversation cannot capture our most profound thoughts and feelings. Rituals give them voice and shape. So, we decorate our Christmas trees, light our menorahs, give gifts, hold hands, and say prayers. What everyday words could we possibly utter that would capture so well our feelings at these moments?

During our time of grief, the very rituals of the holidays can help us survive them.

When we light candles in our homes, we can do so in honor of the person who died. When we sing holiday songs, we can allow ourselves to embrace any grief feelings the music stirs within us. Attending services at our place of worship, praying, and meditating are other meaningful ways to tap into the healing power of ritual this holiday season.

I'm homesick for you. I will look for ways to mourn you during the rituals of the holidays.

DECEMBER 25

*"Christmas—that magic blanket that wraps itself about us, that
something so intangible that it is like a fragrance. It may weave a
spell of nostalgia. Christmas may be a day of feasting, or of prayer,
but always it will be a day of remembrance—a day in which we
think of everything we have ever loved."*

— Augusta E. Rundel

For many of us, Christmas is the pinnacle holiday of the year.
More than any other celebration, it is the day for family and
friends, kindness and generosity. It is the day for love.

Whether we celebrate Christmas or a different significant
holiday at another time of the year, on our special day we
feel the losses that are the counterpoint to our love. There is
missing, yes, but there is also—still and always—the love.

On this day of remembrance, we remember all our loves,
and we are grateful.

*Today I will wrap myself in the magic blanket that is my love for
you. I will express that love in ways it deserves.*

DECEMBER 26

"Life is a beautiful collage of priceless moments and memories, which when pieced all together create a unique, treasured masterpiece."

— Melanie M. Koulouris

Our lives are not paintings that depict a certain scene or tell a single story. Instead, they are great, grand collages—pastiches of hundreds of places, thousands of memories, and millions of moments.

When we are down in the weeds of our collages, they can feel messy and pointless. But when we have the opportunity and wherewithal to step back and view our collages from farther away, we see that they are masterpieces.

I like to think of the people we love as the colors of our collages. Everyone we ever loved gets a color. When we stand back we can see the sunflower yellow of this person throughout this section of our collage and the Tiffany blue of that person in this one special corner. The stronger the attachment, the more that color shows up.

The longer we live, the bigger our collages grow. But the sections we completed with the person who died—those are and will always be essential parts of our unique, treasured masterpieces.

My life has been and will continue to be a beautiful collage of priceless moments and memories.

DECEMBER 27

"Life must be lived forwards, but it can only be understood backwards."
— Søren Kierkegaard

I recently counseled a widower. Eight weeks after his wife's death, his friends told him, "It's time for you to move on." He came to see me because he couldn't reconcile what he was feeling inside with his friends' advice. Needless to say, I affirmed his instinctive need to go backward before going forward. A 44-year-old woman I counseled had a similar experience. This time, just three days (!!!) after her relatively young husband died, a group of women in her neighborhood came to her and said, "We've been talking about you. You're still fairly good looking. We're going to put you on Match.com."

Gah! There is no immediate "Onward!" in grief. There is only the present of our grief and the past of our memories. Oh sure, we still have to get out of bed most days and go about our daily lives, but we don't really march forward. We can't. We shouldn't expect ourselves to—and neither should anyone else, especially in the early weeks and months.

We're looking backward and wallowing in the present of our grief because that's where we need to be right now.

If I'm not ready to move on, I'm not ready to move on.

DECEMBER 28

*"We bereaved are not alone. We belong to the largest company in all
the world—the company of those who have known suffering."*
— Helen Keller

The winter holidays can be so hard for us grievers. They're all
about getting together with the people you love and celebrating,
celebrating, celebrating. But someone we love isn't here to get
together with. And in the middle of an otherwise merry group,
we can feel out of place and somehow even lonelier.

But we bereaved are not alone. Many others are suffering, too.
Let's get together and talk about our grief. Instead of
celebrating, let's mourn together.

Today, start just one conversation with someone else you know
must be silently grieving and see what happens. Defenses
crumble. Walls come down. Mutual healing happens. If we
reach out and actively mourn, the holidays can be for
healing just as much as for celebrating.

*I am not alone in my grief.
I will reach out to another griever today.*

DECEMBER 29

*"The answer to the mystery of existence is the love you shared
sometimes so imperfectly, and when the loss wakes you to the deeper
beauty of it, the sanctity of it, you can't get off your knees for a long
time. You're driven to your knees not by the weight of the loss but by
gratitude for what preceded the loss. And the ache is always there,
but one day not the emptiness, because to nurture the emptiness,
to take solace in it, is to disrespect the gift of life."*

— Dean Koontz

Our loss has awakened us to the sanctity of the love
we shared with those who died.

We are driven to our knees by the pain, yes, but also by our
new understanding of the significance of the relationship. It's
true: We didn't really know what we had until it was gone.

The ache will always be there, though it will lessen through
active mourning. And the emptiness we feel? We must do our
grief work so that we can find ways to fill the emptiness. This is
our task now. This is our sacred responsibility. For to hang onto
the emptiness instead is to die while we are alive and
to disrespect the life of the person who died.

*My loss has awakened me to the gift of love and life.
Doing my grief work honors that gift.*

DECEMBER 30

*"Life is not so much about beginnings and endings as it is about going
on and on and on. It's about muddling through the middle."*
— Anna Quindlen

Death may be a sort of ending for those who have died,
but it's not really an ending for us. We're still here,
muddling through the long middle.

The longer we live, the more we realize that the middle is
peppered with loss—over-peppered, we might say. But still,
in between all the bits of loss is a rich, nutritious broth of
goodness. Embracing our grief means learning to appreciate and
have gratitude for the entire soup, including the peppercorns.

If we're lucky, our middle goes on and on and on. The more we
actively mourn our significant losses, the more deeply
and joyfully we will live out the middle.

*I am learning to not only muddle
through the middle, but muddle well.*

DECEMBER 31

"Hope smiles from the threshold of the year to come
Whispering 'It will be happier.'"
— Alfred Lord Tennyson

Hope is an expectation of a good that is yet to be. It is trust and faith that things can get better. When our presents and pasts are made painful by grief, thank goodness for hope. "Hope is that feeling you have that the feeling you have isn't permanent," famously said playwright Jean Kerr.

In our loving relationships with the people who died, we enjoyed the present, and we also looked forward to the months and years to come. We were present, and we were also hopeful. Wasn't that a wonderful combination?

We can and will regain this synergy of present and future if we commit ourselves to fully and openly mourning our losses.

I resolve to be both present to my grief and hopeful about the year to come.

A FINAL WORD

As you have learned, grief is a one-day-at-a-time journey, but it does not magically "end" after a year. If you have communed with this book throughout the past 365 days and actively explored and expressed all your thoughts and feelings along the way, however, you have also likely experienced a slow, gradual softening of your grief. Grief never truly ends, but it does begin to get easier.

When we actively and authentically mourn our grief, over time we move toward what I call "reconciliation." With reconciliation comes a renewed sense of energy and confidence, an ability to fully acknowledge the reality of the death, and a capacity to become re-involved in the activities of living.

In reconciliation, the sharp, ever-present pain of grief gives rise to a renewed sense of meaning and purpose. Our feelings of loss never completely disappear, yet they soften, and the intense pangs of grief become less frequent. Hope for a continued life emerges as we are able to make commitments to the future, realizing that our loved ones who died will never be forgotten, yet knowing that our lives can and will move forward.

After you complete a full year with this book, you may want to engage with it again the next year. You will find that as you reread and recommit to the meditations, they will speak to you in new and different ways. Or if you've found the book helpful during the past 365 days, you may want to pass it along to someone else who is grieving—along with your reliable and ongoing support.

I wish you peace, love, and much happiness in all the rest of your precious days here on earth.

UNDERSTANDING YOUR GRIEF

Ten Essential Touchstones for Finding Hope and Healing Your Heart

One of North America's leading grief educators, Dr. Alan Wolfelt has written many books about healing in grief. This book is his most comprehensive, covering the essential lessons that mourners have taught him in his three decades of working with the bereaved.

In compassionate, down-to-earth language, Understanding Your Grief describes ten touchstones—or trail markers—that are essential physical, emotional, cognitive, social, and spiritual signs for mourners to look for on their journey through grief.

Think of your grief as a wilderness—a vast, inhospitable forest. You must journey through this wilderness. To find your way out, you must become acquainted with its terrain and learn to follow the sometimes hard-to-find trail that leads to healing. In the wilderness of your grief, the touchstones are your trail markers. They are the signs that let you know you are on the right path. When you learn to identify and rely on the touchstones, you will find your way to hope and healing.

ISBN 978-1-879651-35-7
176 pages • softcover • $14.95

The Ten Essential Touchstones:

Open to the presence of your loss.

Dispel misconceptions about grief.

Embrace the uniqueness of your grief.

Explore your feelings of loss.

Recognize you are not crazy.

Understand the six needs of mourning.

Nurture yourself.

Reach out for help.

Seek reconciliation, not resolution.

Appreciate your transformation.

ALL DR. WOLFELT'S PUBLICATIONS CAN BE ORDERED BY MAIL FROM:
Companion Press | 3735 Broken Bow Road | Fort Collins, CO 80526
(970) 226-6050 | www.centerforloss.com